PRACTICAL
VENTRILOQUISM

BEING

A Thoroughly Reliable Guide to the Art of Voice Throwing and Vocal Mimicry

BY AN ENTIRELY NOVEL SYSTEM OF GRADED EXERCISES

BY

ROBERT GANTHONY

———

WITH NUMEROUS ILLUSTRATIONS

———

Introduction to 1955 Edition

To old-timers Ventriloquism was a mystifying art heard at long intervals on the vaudeville stage. Today Television has given us so many lovable characters whose voices are not their own that its popularity is growing steadily.

Because Mr. Ganthony was one of the old masters who directed his work to those who wish to teach themselves—and we know that so many of you might want to do just that— we decided to reprint his own method from the Original plates.

Mr. Ganthony believed that ventriloquists were not born, but made by the desire to learn and the willingness to practice. Now, ALL that you have to do is PRACTICE!

PREFACE

B^Y Ventriloquism we mean the art, the act, or the practice of speaking or singing in such a manner that the v o i c e appears to come, not from the person himself, but from some other place, as from the opposite side of the room, above or below, etc. A ventriloquist is the performer, the actor.

The author having long been an adept in the art, both as an entertainer and a teacher, feels, that while he may not be filling a long-felt want, he is supplying material for what has proven to be the most popular method of entertaining yet devised. Ventriloquists are not born any more than are musicians. It is only by practice that one can become proficient in anything. Therefore, in laying down the principles necessary in acquiring the art, I feel that all that will be necessary on the part of the student is to practice as often and as long as both time and vocal organs will permit.

Ventriloquism is a healthful exercise even aside from its entertaining feature. If I were a doctor, as I am entertainer, I should prescribe a course in Ventriloquism for all throat and lung troubles. It is also beneficial as a physical exercise for the whole body, for one to be really proficient in the art he must take as much "exercise" as if he were a contortionist or an acrobat.

The system of graduated scales and exercises which I have formulated *create* the Ventriloquial voice by gradually training the vocal organs to an acquaintance with, and a subsequent mastery of the duties required of them.

If this work is to be the means, as it should be, of enabling the reader to astonish and amuse his friends or the public, I shall feel repaid in having indirectly added to that social recreation which enables us to return with greater zest to the more serious duties of every-day life.

VENTRILOQUISM.

PART I.

GENERAL INSTRUCTION.

Introduction.

IN order to be more concise in my directions when
I come to the practical acquirement of Ventriloquism I first allude to the art here in a general
way, contradict accepted fallacies, and dispose of
the astonishing amount of nonsense that has always
been associated with it. If I did not I should be
forced into irritating digression where pertinence
was necessary, or possibly leave the reader to
wonder why I had not told him to do what was
impossible, or allow him to imagine, on the other
hand, that I was inducing him to try and acquire
by cultivation what was solely a natural gift.

The word Ventriloquism, according to its deri-
vitative significance means "speaking from the
belly", but the reader, who may feel some natural
alarm for his digestion, may accept my assurance

that it is nothing of the kind; the stomach has more forcible means of making its wants known than speech.

The Dictionary meaning which best describes it says that it is—" *the imitation of distant sounds.*"

The reader immediately recalls to his mind scores of " Ventriloquists " who never imitated *distant* sounds during their entire entertainment, but simply relied on the proximate vagaries of speech of an assortment of mouth-moving automata to which they supplied conversation.

This anomaly—which I admit—is coeval with the introduction of Ventriloquial Figures, that permit the art of Ventriloquism being eliminated from Entertainments bearing its name; the drolleries of the Figures offering the variety that " voice throwing" did before their invention.

As a matter of fact, there are really *two distinct kinds of Ventriloquism*—" near" and " distant", acquired by methods utterly dissimilar, and being so acquired they become distinct accomplishments, and must be *studied as separate arts* under some such distinguishing title as I have given them.

It is obvious that for purposes of entertainment no ventriloquist would confine himself to the imitation of *distant sounds alone* as his illustrations would lack variety and contrast, so he has cultivated the imitation of near sounds of a grotesque character, and introduced these to set off his distant effects, and these near sounds being merged with the *distant* have come to constitute what was known, even before Figures were thought of, as a Ventriloquial Entertainment.

The "near" Ventriloquism, as I term it, is what the Figure Worker, in the majority of cases, relies upon altogether with which to work his puppets; and precisely the same class of Ventriloquism, ("near") is also used by the Ventriloquist to give variety to his distant effects by proximate sounds, which brings about a confusion of nomenclature which I explain, not to bring disparagement on the Figure Worker who employs "near", nor to give pre-eminence to the Ventriloquist who employs "distant" and "near" but to obtain a necessary classification for purposes of tuition.

The use of the term Ventriloquism for the imitation of near sounds, articulate and inarticulate vocal mimicry and instrumentation is sufficiently correct for the general public, but it is confusing to the student, who, though he may employ them under the common title, must study those he fancies separately as what they are, and blend them together with artistic regard to contrast and effect, when he presents them as a Ventriloquial Entertainment.

The reader may give illustrations of Ventri‧
loquism ("distant") alone if he elect to, "near"
alone, "mimicry, or "instrumentation" alone, and
he could call such illustrations "a Ventriloquial
Entertainment" without fear of contradiction, but,
in this work, I give *all* the varieties, explain
how they should be presented, and it is the
reader's fault if he do not make his entertain‧
ment one in the fullest sense of the term.

An advantage in the classification that I have
adopted I might mention here, which is, that
should the reader's ambition be to *Ventriloquize
with Figures* he can pass over Part I, and com‧
mence at Part II.

If again he wants to imitate an instrument
introduced into a song he can pass over Part I.
and Part II and come to Part III, which remark
would apply should he wish to imitate wood sawing
boiler filling, etc.

My feeling in the matter is that the reader
having bought the book should try the whole
course, which he doubtless will, *as it is only by
doing so that he can discover the extent of his
aptitude and the direction of his talent.*

The reader will not be able, therefore, to decide
at once what sort of Entertainment he can give
best, though he may make a selection, because

he cannot know without a little experimenting what best suits him.

There is no harm in his availing himself of my classification to commence with that for which he has taken a predilection, but I would warn him against purchasing a *lot of Figures* until he is quite certain of what he really intends doing.

The reader cannot do wrong in studying the entire course, because, though he may decide to employ Figures which do not of a necessity demand more than "near" ventriloquism, if he has studied "distant" and "mimicry" his entertainment is enhanced by their introduction, and it certainly is an advantage, if called upon to do some Ventriloquism, to be able to accomplish it with the ordinary assistants of a room, instead of his having to explain that he cannot because he has not brought his dolls with him.

"Distant" Ventriloquism need not necessarily be the imitation of *distant* sounds, as the ventriloquist may imitate a man in a box which gives the same result phonetically.

In working "distant" with Figures he may, under properly arranged provocation, clap his hand on the old man's mouth, when he would use the "distant" voice and make him say as he does so,

'Ere, I can't breathe!"

reverting to "near" as he removes his hand when he would simulate gasping for breath and make the old man say, as he looked at him

" I say, guv'nor, ye nearly smothered me."

Vocal mimicry can be also introduced by the employment of a mechanical Dog, such as is introduced by Leo the well-known Ventriloquist, or vocal Instrumentation by making the Little Girl play a violin, the Nigger a Banjo, or letting the old man imitate Dog, Fiddle, or Banjo.

Voice throwing can be introduced by letting the old man call to his pal on the roof, or by the Ventriloquist at the old man's request giving a few illustrations of Ventriloquism, when the old man interrupts, praises, and criticizes the performance, which arrangement makes it appear to the uninitiated that the Figures' talk is not Ventriloquism, but their real utterances, as you have otherwise the Ventriloquist himself commenting on his own performance.

The reader may wonder why he should use Figures if they can be dispensed with, or why he should not use them if they can be procured.

The advantage of Figures is that they permit the use of a set dialogue, that they amuse the eye as well as the ear, that they make the

Ventriloquist independent of local surroundings, that they do not require so much effort on the part of the performer when entertaining, and that success with them is more easily attained.

The advantages of Ventriloquism without Figures are that the performer is not obliged to carry luggage, that he gives a more artistic form of Entertainment, and is always prepared to give an exhibition of his skill whenever or wherever called upon.

The uncertainty of the surroundings when entertaining makes the unaided Ventriloquist's work difficult.

He may have arranged to give an imitation of a burglary being committed, voices in furtive tones outside the window, after the policeman has been heard saying "good-night" to the cook till his voice has died away in the distance. He intended to have introduced his imitation of sawing wood, breaking glass, etc., and there is no window that he can use!

To show the importance of assistant surroundings let us suppose that the Ventriloquist has a screen by which he stands and uses "near." The onlookers hearing voices and not perceiving that the Ventriloquist moves his lips would conclude that there was someone behind the screen speaking, and further, supposing that the screen

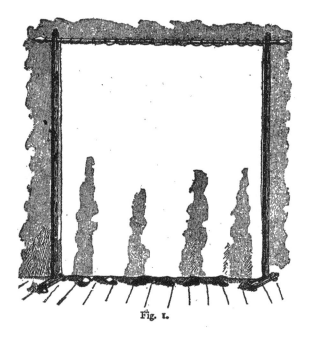

Fig. I.

did not quite touch the ground, and the on-looker perceived feet, he would be still more convinced that someone was there, but turn the screen round and the best ventriloquism would be ineffective!

A question almost invariably put to me after giving illustrations of Ventriloquism takes this form:

Fig. 2.

"Is ventriloquism a gift or can it be acquired?"

The entertainer let loose on a startled society at store prices, or kept in stock on account of his friendship with the clerk of a Bond Street ticket-office, would probably reply with character-istic abandon of modesty: "It is a gift" and leave his questioner to infer that *he* is one of those mortals specially selected by a discriminating providence to exemplify the prodigality of her gifts, and sent by the agent to evidence the moderation of his charges for heaven-born genius in white tie and swallow-tail.

The question is not, however, so easily answered off hand, for it is both in varying proportions.

A "born ventriloquist" is an obvious absurdity! Did anyone ever have, see, or hear of a baby ventriloquist?

I have tried to find one but have not been successful. I have applied personally to the ancestors of ventriloquists but have not succeeded in discovering the progenitors of this rara avis. Unfortunately the early histories of the majority of professors of this art are so involved in obscurity that statistics are difficult to obtain.

I have interviewed my old nurse, who knew my mother before I did, and she says that though I would eat coal whenever opportunity presented itself I never did any ventriloquism in the early stages of my career. If I wanted food, or a pin hurt me I intimated the fact to the household, and the neighbourhood generally in an unmistakeable manner, but *I did not employ ventriloquism.*

It would naturally take a baby longer to learn this art than an adult because it must first learn to talk—just as it must first walk before it can skate, and crawl before it can walk.

The duckling that swam, or the chicken that could peck directly it broke the shell and emerged from the egg, never were and never will be hatched, any more than the baby will be born who announces its entry into the world by giving a ventriloquial entertainment to its astonished parents and their medical attendant.

I shall therefore compliment the intelligence of the reader by assuming that he admits the absurdity of the born Ventriloquist theory, and that he will allow me to substitute for this fallacy such instruction as will enable him to become one by study and practice.

As it would be equally absurd to deny that natural aptitude and qualification do not also exist, I shall descend to the common or garden simile and say that you cannot get anything from a mine without digging for it, you may find gold, silver, slate, or useless earth, but you must *dig* to know what your mine really contains. The mine is your physical qualifications and, as good engineering and energy develop the resources of a mine, so will assiduity and good instruction develop your vocal organs and gain you the best results from your mine of possible ventriloquy.

It is precisely the same with Ventriloquism as with any other art, but so persistently is this " nascitur" versus "fit" question put to me in my professional experience that I am sure it is the question the reader will require me to answer before he settles down to gain by study that Ventriloquial proficiency which is not his nor anyone else's by inheritance.

I must be pardoned if I appear to dwell at too great length on this point, but I must upset generally accepted theories I know to be erroneous and establish the fact that Ventriloquism is an *acquired* art, otherwise there is no reason or service in half this volume.

Whatever success is obtained, even by the so-called born Ventriloquist, *it is obtained by some sort of practice*, essay, experiment or what he please to call it. Attempts are made to throw the voice—to make it sound at a distance, nearer, below, above and he continues such attempts until he discovers how to produce the effects he requires *all of which attempts are virtually a training to acquire ventriloquial speech.*

In this groping after what should be attained scientifically the throat will suffer, however, and the vocal organs will be needlessly injured.

Though the reader may want to ventriloquize

at once by the mere revelation of a secret, such a thing is impossible.

There is no royal road to learning anything, and it must be patent to anyone that it is much more sensible to adopt an approved course of study that offers the most rapid attainment of the art without injury, than to flounder about in blundering experiments that are certain to harm the vocal organs and equally certain to produce an imperfect and unsatisfactory ventriloquial result.

How to become a Ventriloquist.

BY Ventriloquism, as I use it in an unqualified sense, I mean the power of imitating distant sounds and in teaching you—I will ask permission to use the second person instead of the third while instructing—you become under this heading a Ventriloquist in the true and original sense of the term.

The quality of a distant sound is that it is *distant*, not a near sound made *piano*. It is a sound obtainable by placing the vocal organs in a certain position. If I described that position surgically you could not achieve it, because, even if you understood the terms I employed, you have no power over the organs mentioned to fix them as you desired.

I will at the risk of being indelicate give you
such advice as cannot be misunderstood, and
which, if followed, must place your vocal organs
in the position they should be for Ventriloquism.

"The Ventriloquial Drone."

To acquire this take a deep breath and holding
it make a reaching sound at the back of the
throat, as though trying to be sick, as you do
this utter a prolonged "ah" exhaling slowly.

The "ah" will at first be a grunt, but try
again making a greater effort to produce a reaching
sound prolonging the "ah"—when it begins to sound
like an uncertain drone—and finally settles down
to a *sustained clear hum like that of a distant
bee drone*, from which it derives its name. The
further back in the throat the sound is made the
more distant will it appear to the listener, and
the more forward in the throat it is made the
nearer will it appear to the listener.

You may not get the Ventriloquial drone at once
but you will with a little practice. *When you
hear that clear drone you may know that you have
your mouth as it should be for Ventriloquism*
but until you do produce that you must hark
back and try again, because, *unless this foundation is laid properly all that follows is unsatis-*

factory 'and your ventriloquism will lack that distant quality to obtain which is to be a Ventriloquist.

Practice on the bee drone enables you to *sustain the vocal chords in position* and familiarises them with their novel and unnatural duties.

When you hear a man throw his voice and it wavers about, the effect is unnatural, and shows that he has gained his knowledge haphazardly, for, by practice of the drone and scales the requisite command is obtained, and this uncertainty avoided, as is also avoided that painful straining which results from an ignorance of how to produce the distant quality of sound required.

When you have acquired the drone, *and know it is right,* you will be inclined to attempt voice-throwing with vocabulary, etc. Your success will probably surprise you and lead you wrong, so don't—at least don't do much at present or you will do harm.

The acquirement of the " Drone" is the acquirement of all distant sounds.

To illustrate this at once you shall imitate distant sheep but once for all *whatever you imitate, imitate nature.* In imitating a bee vou imitate the sustained hum of the insect's rapidly beating wings. It is a continued sound only altering as the insect approaches or recedes, but in imitating a flock of sheep you imitate a number of sheep, each with a different sound, made in a different locality, some following quickly on others, some after a pause. In making the bee drone approach it must be done gradually, in fact at the rate a bee progresses. With sheep it may or may not be a sudden change of distance, as when a ewe bleats near to you and a lamb at some distance replies, or when a number of sheep near bleat almost together.

If you substitute for the prolonged "ah" of the bee the short "bah" of the sheep you will find no difficulty in giving the effect of sheep outside a window or in the remote distance.

Rooks.

THE principle of imitating a flock of rooks is akin to the imitation of sheep. We are accustomed to hear both in flocks, with this difference, that the rook, for reasons of his own, is usually heard only at a distance, and the sound when you become more skilful should be an overhead as well as a distant sound. It is these niceties that raise Ventriloquism to an art and charm the listener. The method of throwing the voice overhead will be found fully explained later on,

I do not introduce it here, as I am only now illustrating the value of the "Drone" in it simplest form.

"Dogs, Cock, etc."

IF you can mimic the sound of a dog barking near you have only to assume the "drone" position to make the sound appear outside (distant) and the same with the crow of a cock.

Drone vowel practice.

THOUGH "ah" or â is the most useful vowel. as will be seen by the foregoing distant imitations, it is insufficient alone when we imitate speech which of course employs all the vowels. If you merely practice on "ah" and then employ speech without practising equally on the other vowels your illustrations will be imperfect, because you will have but an imperfect command over the unpractised vowels. Instead of droning on "ah" substitute the other vowels, until they become equally easy to produce and sustain.

Echo practice.

THIS is to obtain a sudden transition from "Vent:" to "natural;" from its resemblance to an echo, its study is so named.

Commence by saying "Ah!" "natural" following it by "ah!" "Vent:" not as a prolonged drone but staccato fashion, and practice this with all the vowels.

This practice enables you to give with ease those effects, where, for instance, you speak to someone outside a window, one voice "natural" is your natural one, the other is the Vent: and the change from one to another must be rapidly and constantly made, which facility is obtained by "echo" practice.

The principle you will notice is one observed in singing when the vowels are used instead of words for practice. If you avoid words your faculties are all centred on obtaining proper contrast and your vocal chords learn their duties without being disturbed by the business of the tongue and lips, and a much more satisfactory result is obtained. When words are added the effect is heightened, but, if words are introduced at first, they only deceive the student in regard to his progress.

Having secured the distant effect with the vowels in close contrast to the near, substitute "Hullo" for vowels, and the effect of an echo is increased, not because you have suddenly improved your ventriloquism, but because "Hullo" is the natural

way of testing an echo. At an earlier stage this
would satisfy you even though imperfectly done
and prevent you excelling in the ventriloquial
effect, as you would be satisfied with the dialogue
effect, and to your untrained ear the "Hullo"
with the Vent: acquired by drone would be good
enough to deter you from further effort. When
I say "you" I am addressing the average pupil
as he appears to me from my experience. There
are pupils who prefer to secure the ventriloquial
effect before they use vocabulary, but they are
not in a majority, for nearly all want to paint
before they can draw.

In making the Vent: reply you will find that
you cannot aspirate the H in "Hullo" so do not
attempt to, nor feel disappointed if you cannot.
The possibilities of Ventriloquial dialogue are
treated of in their place under "vocabulary" so that
a passing reference is all that is necessary here

"Above" to "Level."

It is a very common thing for Ventriloquists
to remark, after throwing the voice to the roof,
that "the man can't get down because he has
no ladder." This is not the real reason, which
is that the Ventriloquist wants a little instruction.
He has gained his effect by accident, and, not

understanding the instrument he is playing on his technique is limited and like the self-taught fiddler he never gets beyond the " first position." This always seems to me a pity both for the public, and the performer, to say nothing of the art itself.

Although I have tested this matter before, 1 remove my cigar from my mouth as I am writing and throw my voice to the room above and the sound *is there.* There appears an isolation, if I may use the term, between the voice above and myself sitting at my desk. I have not used the Drone pure and simple though I have retained the Vent: formation of the vocal organs. I have used the Vent: method and so produced the distant effect, but, instead of the back production I have forced the sound against the back of the hard palate, see fig. 3, this makes the sound appear to come from above,—as you make this sound you can feel the percussion of the sound striking the palate—and as the voice descends from "above" to "level," you send the sound against and round the back of the mouth (figures 1, 2, 3 and 4).

This is extremely interesting to the student, as it shows that what is done in the mouth is reproduced in effect, and though like a magic lantern, the picture is enlarged on reproduction, it must

Fig. 3.

be properly placed in the lantern as the sound must be properly placed in the mouth.

As you think of the man coming down—and always do think of him—so project the sound against the top and back of the mouth until your "above" descends to the ordinary drone position when the voice will sound on a level with you and be what I designate "Level."

You will find after practice that you have a diapason of from five notes to an octave which constitutes the "Above to Level", which diapason must be secured by scale exercise with the ordinary drone. You commence with "ah" but instead of producing it unreverberated at the back of the throat you reverberate it against the top and subsequently against the top back, and back of mouth as I have indicated. To obtain this " above " sound practise " ah " and then on the other vowels without distracting your attention with vocabulary.

If you try speech, to see how you progress, there is no harm in that, but do not *practice with speech at first.*

Dialogue "above" to "level".

Vent:	*" Jack! Jack! Jack ! "
Jack:	"' Ullo! " (above)
Vent:	*" Are you there? Are you there? *'
Jack :	" No, I'm 'ere"
Vent:	" Will you come down, please ? You'll find a ladder—I say you'll find a ladder. "
Jack:	" All right. Keep yer 'air on—I've got it. "

Note—As a rule be more loquacious in your natural voice than in the Vent: voice, it is less fatiguing, and the audience appreciate most that of which they get least.

Vent:	" Come along "
Jack:	*All right I'm coming down now."

" I'm coming down now *" is repeated as the voice is brought down. It is a suitable sentence

* The name is repeated as though calling to some one, pausing after first "Jack", and speaking sharply for third, and so with repeated sentences.

for the purpose and its simple repetition is best, because the listener is amused at the descent of the voice, and not at what is being said. The "come along" of the Vent: always the same pitch, acts as a foil to the other.

Jack: "Oi be down now."

Vent: "That's all right,"

which two sentences when level is reached would, for instance, finish the illustration.

In *singing* the "above" to "level" drone, my voice gives this scale, but the first five notes

only are really quite satisfactory.

When the "above" to "level" is secured the voice must be made to descend below. In *entertaining*, the change of position of the vocal organs, necessary to allow the man to continue his journey into the cellar, is covered by suitable business at the door, or window as hereafter illustrated.

"Level" to "Below".

THE principle is the same as the "above to level" but more difficult to explain. Forget that you know anything about the "above" voice, and begin with the "Level" stretching your

neck out to its natural length, and as you wish
the voice to sound lower shorten your neck until
your chin rests on your chest. Practise this with
three notes on " ah " making the sound *down the
throat and not against the palate.*

The stomach is drawn up with the " Below "
voice more than with the " above " and the vocal
chords appear to me to be so compressed that
the sound is prevented from rising and the downward effect is produced by it being forced down
the throat. This is in substance what I said
before, that the sound is directed by the vocal
organs to where it is desired to be simulated,
the muffled sound of Ventriloquism representing
distance while the projection of sound in mouth
suggests direction.

When I say stretch the neck and press the
bottom of the chin against the chest to obtain
" Level " to " Below," I say this to try and transfer
my meaning through print, as when I suggested
sickness to start the " Drone " correctly. In
actual practice no contortions are necessary nor
permissible.

Level to Distant Level.

If the voice is required to go away on a level
the means taken to produce the " above " and

"below" voices are avoided, and you neither speak against the palates nor down the throat, but compress the chords and throw the voice backwards. "Good-night" is the best sentence for this effect "good-morning or evening" being unworkable. I might mention that in saying "good-night" your own voice becomes louder as the Vent: voice grows fainter, and the pauses between the salutations are longer, as would happen were the effect produced naturally, until at last you would yell, and the reply would be inaudible.

Possibilities of Voice-throwing.

THIS is a matter upon which there is a good deal of misconception. With the exception of a yard or so towards the listener, *the Ventriloquist must come between the sound he imitates and the listener.*

The following diagram will explain the limits of voice-throwing. V represents the Ventriloquist, L the listener, and the figures 1 to 16 the extent to which the art of voice throwing is possible.

From 1 to 12 the voice can be thrown until it becomes inaudible, from 13 to 16 if you attempt to throw it more forward it becomes yours, and returns to you. If the Vent: voice be thrown forward, or follows 1 to 12 *in a close radius* it

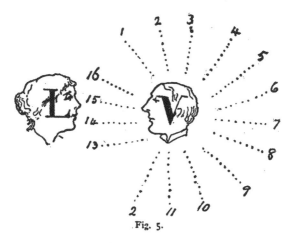

Fig. 5.

must be thrown into a box behind walls or inside a listener, etc., as it is obvious, that if you use a Vent: or distant voice it must either be subdued by the effect of distance, or covered to suggest that effect. To throw the voice forward and not suggest a reason for the Vent: voice would be unnatural, as any voice *nearer* to the audience than your own would be *louder*.

So many experiments can be given that astonish people, that it is not necessary to explain its limits to an audience but show its capabilities.

Resumé.

You have now the capacity of imitating distant,

sounds, the art which originally gave rise to the term " Ventriloquism."

You can throw your voice to a room above to a cellar below, and do this without undue effort, also make the voice gradually descend from roof to cellar or go away on a level until it is heard no more.

By this art, as I have said, distant sounds are imitated. There are many that I have not men tioned as there will be many that you will discover for yourself. I might instance the sound of a stone thrown on the ice, the first blow it strikes, and then the sound of each bound as it goes away till it slides along at last and finally stops.

Should Ventriloquial practice make your throat ache, the remedy is simple. *Do not use it ven- triloquially for a time.* Don't practise when you have a cough. Gargle with cold water with or without a little sea salt added.

I next treat of the imitation of near articulate sounds as employed in Ventriloquism and so begin to build up the materials for an Entertainment

PART II.

NEAR VENTRILOQUISM.

Introduction.

CHATTING recently about Ventriloquism with Lord Mountmorres, he said, "I prefer, then, what you term near Ventriloquism." It is very unusual for anyone to say that, so I asked him, "Why?" and he replied, "That in Ventriloquism distant or voice throwing there seems to be only one voice heard,—that of a countryman, and this man is always the individual who climbs up on the roof, wanders below, or ultimately with a volubility of salutation retires into oral obscurity. But with near Ventriloquism you can introduce more variety and, so it appears to me, create more amusement.

I quote his remarks without permission, because they suggest themselves as being an apposite introduction to this portion of my subject.

The Vent: voice may be an Irishman's but perhaps until the Home Rule Bill is passed the Irishman may be considered a *countryman*, and so the remark I have quoted holds good.

There is, however, no variety in the character of the Vent: voice as is explained under vocabulary.

In near Ventriloquism we employ what might be termed character voices, but what more nearly approach caricature voices. To attain them is easier than to attain the Vent: voice, though, like it, a certain position of the mouth must be acquired by practice.

In order to deceive the listener more completely, exaggerated voices are used that differ entirely from your own, voices that would never come from a gentleman's lips. These voices *are not thrown but their locality is suggested by acting* with the assistance of screens or curtains, or by the employment of talking Figures.

The acting necessary for near Ventriloquism where the voice is *not* thrown, does not prove that when it is thrown acting is employed instead of Ventriloquism. It is this that leads to confusion in the general mind, but the student, understanding the subject, will prove to an audience that acting is not a substitute for voice throwing, when he gives illustrations of Ventriloquism, and having

done so uses all his artifice to lead them to believe
that he throws his voice when employing " near "
by expression and gesture. The public must be
humbugged a little or it doesn't like it.

Ventriloquial Figures are used in proximity to
the Entertainer, the moving mouths of which and
the still lips of the performer make the illusion
absolute, especially on a stage.

If the reader incline to use Figures he need
not study Ventriloquism, as the " near " will be
all that is really necessary to give a successful
Entertainment, say with two knee dolls, which he
could do with less than a month's practice, and with
less strain to the vocal chords.

As a boy I could not understand why if I
could make D with my third finger on the A
string I should require to make it with my first
when playing the violin. The reason is much
the same as learning varieties of Ventriloquism
and that is, for additional effect as when "near"
will do to serve for entertaining without Figures
one also adds " distant."

The attainment of near Ventriloquism is not
merely using natural speech with still lips, it is
a more accentuated speech than character speech
as we should understand it on the stage; so I
have termed it " caricature " speech which requires,

though in a modified form, the same class of training as is required for Ventriloquism.

Caricature Voices.

THAT piercing female voice, which in Ventriloquism is supposed to represent mature womanhood, is obtained by the cultivation of what is termed the "punch voice." This voice like the "Drone" is utilized for numerous effects in addition to the speech of the querulous old woman. The squeaking of a door, imitation of reed instruments, the metallic sound of a mandoline string, crowing of a Bantam, parrot, child, cat, lamb, etc.

To command this quality you practise

The Theeek Voice.

PLACE the tongue against the back of the front teeth of the upper jaw and say Th-ê-ê-ê-k prolonging the e's and thinking as you do so of a swiss pipe, a squeaking door, the upper notes of a clarionet.

It is important to get the right quality into the THEEEK voice, because you must produce by its practice a voice that startles with its strangeness. I try myself to fail to get the sound when following my own directions but I cannot.

so conclude they are correct.' I have referred to the sound being like the sound of a reed instrument, and it is not only like it but is made in the same way. If you play a clarionet you press the reed with your mouth before it will sound, and so you press your tongue against your teeth and palate and produce the sound in a manner identical to the production of the instrument and containing in consequence the same quality of sound.

The "punch" voice of the streets is produced by a "call" being placed in the mouth, but the character is the same. *

Try the following dialogue at a curtain.

> *Vent:* "You may not be aware of it, ladies and gentlemen, but there is an old woman behind this curtain.
>
> *O. L.* "What do you call me?" (*using punch voice.*)
>
> *Vent:* "An old lady, I should say."
>
> *O. L.* "That's better."
>
> *Vent:* "I want you to sing." (*putting arm behind curtain.*)
>
> *O. L.* "Take your arm away—I know what you are."

A further illustration might be given of the boy who puts leaf in his mouth.

Vent.   "I was only—"

O. L.   "Yes I know all about it so don't do
          it again."

Vent: "Will you sing?"

O. L.   "Yes, I'll sing out, if you put your
          arm round my—eh?—oh, I did not
          know there was anyone there." (*Sings.*)

> "I dreamt that I dwealt in marbil 'alls,
> With tassels and scarfs by my side—"

Vent: "Vassals and serfs."

O. L.   "Tassels and scarfs."

Vent: "Vassals and serfs."

O. L.   "Tassels and scarfs."

Vent: "Vassals and—"

O. L.   "If you know so much you'd better
          sing it yourself."

If you are not satisfied with your old woman's
voice, or the audience are not, revert to the
"Theeek" practice, prolonging the Theeek and
making it reedy and metallic until you impart
this quality without effort, to any Ventriloquial
dialogue or imitation that requires it. I don't
want you to practice "Theeek" a moment more
than is necessary, because such practice is irksome,
and for that reason it is apt to be passed over
and discarded before the voice is formed; its
employment, as it were, creates, but I want it

practised until it can be used with vocabulary without losing its character. As a contrast to the punch voice we use the

Grunt Voice.

THE tongue lies flat and the whole of the vocal chords lie loose, and less effort is made to speak than would be made naturally, as the words are simply grunted at the back of mouth, the lips are still, and only the back of the tongue is used, the tip lying still at the back of the front lower teeth.

The voice is a caricature of old men you hear sometimes, who have lost command over tongue and lips and speak with open mouths.

The grunt voice is used either with Figures, to supply speech for "old man" in contrast to the reedy sharp voice of "old woman," or for the same purpose when the same couple are suggested behind a screen. These two form the staple fun in Figure working, as, however many Heads or Figures are introduced, these two voices are used most continuously.

Ghostly Voice.

THIS is the grunt without the grunt, a sort of hoarse whisper—a voice destroyed by chronic hoarseness and drink. It is effective in suggesting the loafer and cadger, and it only requires a little suitable dialogue at a partially opened door to suggest to people in a room that you have outside the cadger of the street corners trying to beg, borrow or steal.

I said partially opened door because you cannot ventriloquize a whisper. This voice is not a countryman's—nature does not permit the necessary degradation the ownership of this voice necessitates—the character of voice is the product of large cities.

Little Girl.

FOR this we revert to the punch voice only if possible do not make the voice too reedy, but like a child's. A child, or in fact the young of all animals, uses a high key to speak or make the sound peculiar to itself. A lamb's bleat only changes when the lamb becomes full-grown, so the Little Girl's is much higher than the Woman's Voice, though the punch voice is employed for both.

There is a certain kind of very reedy-voiced Little Girl that Ventriloquists employ with one set of jokes and humorous business, you can either copy that Little Girl, jokes and all, or proceed in a more artistic way, and imitate from nature any child that suits your purpose.

Negro.

THE characteristic "e-yah" laugh, and style is so well known, or can be so easily studied from the burnt-cork minstrels, that I need not refer to it at length here.

Yankee, Frenchman, etc.

These imitations really become dialect studies and it would be impossible to refer to them all. The accepted Yankee should have the twang he inherits from the early puritans; he "guesses" and "calculates;" indulges in exaggerated humour in which death and physical injury are relied upon to provoke mirth. The Frenchman lacks in aspirates what he makes up for in r's; gives a sex to everything, and introduces a little theeek quality into terminations ending in n. The German puts a b where he should use a p and vice versa, a v for a w; but there are enough Germans in America to enquire from or imitate.

PART III.

ENTERTAINING.

THE preceding instructions enable you to Ventriloquize and imitate near voices in caricature which, as far as speech is concerned, is all that you require. To amalgamate this knowledge and to produce a natural effect, or what is a humorous travesty of nature, is the next step towards giving an Entertainment. To utter sounds with an unmoved countenance is another, and the requisite subtlety and device necessary to Ventriloquial acting, is again another, as is also a proper selection of vocabulary.

If I had bothered you to keep your lips still when you were learning to throw the voice, the labial and the vocal studies would have interfered with each other, and the requisite concentration of mind would not have been secured. and you would not have learnt to think in your throat and been able to move the soft palate, tongue, etc., as you now can your fingers. Doing one thing at a time is a good rule for Ventriloquism, and the bundle is easily broken if it be undone and each stick taken in turn. We will now learn the art of

Entertaining.

THE first essential to deception, that is to induce the listener to absolve you from participation in the voices behind screens, or that proceed from the mouth of automata, is to acquire.

Speech with still lips.

THE unguided student in this matter gives himself a lot of unnecessary trouble because he does not start with the knowledge that *only a selected vocabulary can be spoken without moving the lips.* He hears a Ventriloquist with still lips carry on a duologue or triologue, his critical faculties are not sufficiently trained for him to perceive how carefully the labials are expunged. He will return home and practice and of a cer- tainty use words that are impracticable, and which, however much he practise, he could never succeed in uttering, he becomes disheartened, and con- cludes that he "hasn't the gift," or something of that sort. Let him try and say without moving his lips-

" The persistent pertinacity of the priesthood."

And he will not be satisfied with his progress if he try for a century. If on the other hand he try such a sentence as—

"All right, guv'nor, I'm there to-morrow. Good-night to you," he will find no difficulty. One of the first things to do in not moving the lips is to avoid such words that cannot be pronounced without doing so, and then to learn to prevent them moving,—as they will do—when they are not absolutely necessary to articulation. A free use of the lips, tongue, etc., give clearness of speech. The squeaky voice, the indistinct "grunt" can all be produced by a false placement of the vocal organs, and in most cases I should say defective speech like round shoulders is the result of slovenliness.

Practise before a glass and arrange such phrases as do not require labial pronunciation, until you can employ Ventriloquism, or "near" without change of countenance.

When you speak in your natural voice you employ as much as possible words that are restricted in Ventriloquism, which helps to conceal the art.

When you cease to speak naturally your countenance changes as though you had really ceased, although you are still sustaining a conversation.

After a time the face changes by habit when you drop the natural voice.

In closing the lips it is not necessary to close the teeth, as I have seen some performers do, which gives them the appearance of a Russian Cossack in active warfare, but it is best to partially do so, which gives a natural and pleased expression to the face. If the mouth be too much open the movements of the tongue are seen. If the teeth are clenched the tongue is not seen, but the sound cannot leave the mouth, so a middle course must be adopted, to which end a mirror can direct you better than I can.

There are times during an Entertainment when it is possible to use the lips, such as when the business permits you turning your head away from the audience. These chances should be seized upon and the proscribed words used vigorously.

If you pick anything up from the floor your head is down so the old man might say:—

"*Please, Pick up that Pin, guv'nor.*"

As you have for years been moving your lips when you speak, you must not be impatient if you cannot drop the habit at once.

Ventriloquial Acting.

THIS like the negative adjunct of speaking with still lips and countenance is an important aid to entertaining, and the sustaining of an illusion when carrying on an imaginary conversation. If I say that Ventriloquial acting is a difficult form of the histrionic art, the actor will laugh at the idea as readily as the general public conclude that Ventriloquism *is only acting.* The latter I put in the dark room for enlightenment and the former I give in more detail the reasons for my statement.

Having been principal comedian to some of our leading actors:—the late Chas. Calvert (sit tibi terra levis), a member of Henry Irving's Lyceum Co., of Edward Terry's Co., etc., etc., I am in a position to form an opinion on the subject, as I know what ordinary acting is, and what Ventriloquial acting is also.

When for instance Mr. Irving, as Mathias in "The Bells," said to me: "You bled me—that was enough," I had only to look—while acting the Doctor—the medical ass I certainly felt, but had I been acting Ventriloquially I should have had to say to myself with the necessary intonation: "You bled me" etc., and instead of being able to express in my face what I said I must express what I heard though I myself said it, which is certainly more complex. You have Ventriloquial acting when Mr. Cole with an expression of nervous enquiry examines the mechanical arrangements of his Figures.

This *is acting* because Mr. Cole is too experienced an Entertainer to come before the public with faulty automata. His anxiety and solicitude are assumed, and so far he acts as an actor would act, but he makes the old man watch him, and to do this, to follow his own movements with the head of the old man, he must have a dual imagination at work, which is required in a fuller extent when the old man appears to catch his master's anxiety, and says in a whisper heard all over the house: "'As my string broke, guv'nor?" 'or when Mr. Cole, while acknowledging some deserved plaudit by an obeisance, causes the old man to inform the stalls that the Figures are only made of wood.

When Mr. Le Hay, another clever Figure worker has accomplished some effect; his "old man" looks up, and then, turning to those near, says: "I wonder how the little devil does it!"

The gravity of the Ertertainer's face when using ventriloquy is, in my estimation, more creditable to an actor, than to a ventriloquist. who has made that his sole study, because in acting the actor trains his face to express what he says, or what is supposed to be passing through his mind. the Ventriloquist does not express what he says by facial expression unless he speaks in propriâ personâ. His speech may include several voices in rapid succession, voice throwing and a sudden resumption to his own voice, compelling him to appropriately act the listener while working each Figure, and make them listen to him as far as movements permit. which demonstrates the intricate nature of Ventriloquial acting.

I do not imply that the acting of the Ventriloquist is to be compared to the histrionic delineation of great characters, because to successfully portray them the actor must be intellectually great himself. and the few who do succeed make their art the highest form of Entertainment possible. But I do say that to execute difficult ventriloquial feats, with appropriate gesture and with natural facial replies to the remarks of the voices created. is as difficult of attainment as acting is in the ordinary way.

Acting in Ventriloquism is of the greatest value, and by not confusing it with Ventriloquism

itself it can be studied as acting. In acting you
should imagine that you are the person ·you
assume to be, and that you behave as that person
would under the circumstances in which you are
placed by the Author. If the characterisation of
the author is consistent,—the result is a faithful
representation of nature, and is in consequence successful. Without acting, Ventriloquism loses' its
entertaining character, just as a conjuring entertainment does, and becomes merely vocal or
manual trickery, and though the audience are
amazed, the effect is not so complete, so tho-
roughly enjoyable, as if, while being amazed, they
are at the same time charmed by the manner in
which what amazes them is presented.

If I had two pupils one who excelled in Ventriloquism, but who was a poor actor, the other
a good actor but not so successful a ventriloquist,
the latter, when it came to entertaining, would
probably become *the more popular* with the
public.

When you speak in propriâ personâ, to the
audience, and your remarks are followed by Ventriloquy to which you listen, it is as well to
exaggerate your natural expression so that your
features, by contrast, appear more absolutely in
repose afterwards, and thus people infer, without

troubling to analyse their inference, that you do not make the sound you Ventriloquize with still lips because, when you did speak, your face moved in response to your speech. There are times, however, when it is more important to assume an emphatic expression of anger, surprise, or pleasure in response to your Ventriloquy in order to accentuate it, and permit its full enjoyment by the audience.

If the illustrations, for example, are of distant birds, you assume while Ventriloquizing an attitude of interested attention, made more noticeable by having introduced your subject with full expression of countenance while speaking. On the other hand, supposing that you are about to provoke some comic retort from the "man outside." You introduce the illustration in a serious gentlemanly way, so that his impertinence comes with sharper contrast, and your exaggerated expression of anger, etc., is more effective because not indulged in previously.

. In receiving an impertinent answer your annoyance will make the audience laugh, but remember, that although you make the reply and consequently know what it is, you must act as though you heard it for the first time when it is spoken, and you must hear it first, understand it and

then illustrate by your expression how it affects
you. The lady on the stage who opens a letter
and exclaims the whole contents before she could
have read the address, must not be copied.

After practice you cease to believe that Ventriloquial speech is your own, but imagine that
the Little Girl does speak, that the man or woman
are behind the screen or that there is a man
outside, and further than that by exercise of the
imagination you create strongly marked individu-
ality as well as vocal peculiarity in your people,
and their replies become as characteristic as their
tones of voice. The old lady is a virago, and
the old man is consequently always snubbed by
her, or the child may domineer, or the father
and mother be too fond of exercising their parental
authority. Whatever family arrangements are
decided on they must be adhered to all through,
and the audience will recognize the consistency
of their humour.

In using Figures you need not *imagine* that
they are there, because *they are there*, but you
imagine *they* speak and you furnish them with
characters, you humour them, reprimand them,
and *think, hear and see for them.* As soon as
you become accustomed to Figures your hands
fall into position to move their heads and mouths

and the instant you manipulate the old man, your vocal organs are as ready to supply him with speech as your brain is to invent it. Some Ventriloquists stand behind their Figures as stolid as if they too were wood, but this is not an artistic method, as, with it, acting is dispensed with and the entertainer might just as well be hidden behind a rag as the punch and judy man, whom he imitates, for all the assistance he renders optically.

In my own show I walked on to the stage, and appeared surprised and pleased to find it already occupied, shook hands with the old man (whose arm moved) and heard from him how they had all come down by train, the discomforts of travelling in a box and then, from that introduction, mixed myself with the Figures and got to work.

To come on to the stage, bow, examine the strings and then explain that you intend to give a Ventriloquial Entertainment, is a style of proceeding that worries me for days afterwards; it is so "*not how to do it.*"

Ventriloquial acting without Figures is somewhat more intricate and demands more resource on the part of the performer than when he employs these amusing assistants and the performer who arranges his own dialogue must use his imagination as a play-wright does, or should do, always preserving in his mind that he is acting a little comedy, all the characters of which are merely heard, one of which himself alone is seen, an arrangement the average actor-manager would consider dramatic paradise.

May I illustrate this?

Vent: "Ventriloquism, ladies and gentlemen, some say is a gift, so it is, that is, if you pay those you employ when you humbug the public into believing you can throw your voice. I will let you hear me throw my voice into the garden. It is raining, but my remarks are so dry that"—(*at side of blind and to someone outside*)—"Are you there?"

— "All right, I'm 'ere."

Vent: "Will you sing?" (*with back to audience at window.*)

—. Sings: "I love a pretty girl, 'er name is Bella. I wish as 'ow I'd got her new umbrella."

(The Vent.'s back is turned so he uses the word "pretty," and his lips to their fullest extent. The attitude is a natural one, as any-ne would

go to a window to speak to a person outside. If the Vent: did not, his work, however good, would be less effective.)

Vent: "Very clever song but very short."

— "Long enough before you 'ear it again"

Vent: (*carelessly turns a slot of the blind, as he does the voice outside exclaims simultaneously with the action,*)

— "Oh, there's a pretty girl—who's that old chap with the bald head," etc.

(The Vent: has in his opening address noticed any prominent object animate or inanimate, which he alludes to as he adopts the man's voice outside and moves the slot. The exclamation of the man on getting a peep into the room is quite natural if we allow him to be there at all, as are also his impertinent remarks on the company. The Vent:'s back being turned the illusion is increased, as it is not suggested that he is looking into the room, and the idea that he has previously noticed what he intended to remark upon does not occur to the audience. He closes slot annoyed at the remarks from outside and the voice immediately says:

— "You needn't shut the door in my face that way, guv'nor."

4

Vent: *(To audience)* "I am distressed beyond measure to have subjected you to these impertinent remarks, but it is so difficult to get men of immaculate manners to assist me in my Entertainments that"—*(with hand behind him Vent: knocks at window)* "What is it?" *(turns)*

— "Oi be a-comin' in."

Vont: *(Getting under venetian blinds)* "No."

— "Oi says yes Oi be a-comin' in."

Vent: *(Louder)* "No, you can't come in you are not dressed.'

— "Do you think oi got no clothes on?'

Vent: "Your boots are muddy—you can't come in."

— "Oi be coming in."

Vent: "No."

— "Yes, Oi be *(raise window and use near gruff voice)* Oi be comin' in.

Vent: *(As if pushing him out. The blind shakes about and looks as if there was someone trying to get in at the open window, then loud voice, struggle.)*

— "Here's the dog, I must come in.

Vent: " No."

—   " Yes."

Vent: , 'No."   *(Push, shut down window).*
"I say, guv'nor, you got my
thumb in the window,* *(open window
and shut it)* oh, don't it hurt! *(bark
distant)* here's the toy terrier comin',
good-night, good-night."

*(The good-night and bark die away in the
distance and the Entertainer emerges from the
blinds and if he has done his work cleverly he
will get well applauded.)*

In this illustration we have Ventriloquism but
also in my opinion, if I may refer in terms of
approval of my own work, an artistic presentation
which sets it off.

In making allusions in reference to the audience
as instanced by the man peeping through the
opened slot, you must exercise judgment in
what you say, so as not to offend. If a man
appear further removed from the monkey tribe
than his fellow creatures by having a bald head,
this fact is usually supposed to be by the ordinary humorist a matter for ridicule, rather than

---

* It is scarcely necessary to explain that the " gruff near" voice
is only used when the window is open, the Ventriloquist's "distant"
voice when the glass intervenes as window is closed

congratulation, and although I have suggested this
remark, it is only because it is exactly what a
low-class man would allude to, baldness with
him, being a greater crime than drinking.

If he says "there be a pretty girl" the remark
though accepted universally by all the young
ladies present will annoy nobody.

In this matter you must be guided by circumstances.

The responsive acting to the Little Girl should
suggest that the person being spoken to is a
little girl. The manner is gentler, the language
simpler than when you address the "old man."
It is all these little niceties of detail that sustain
an illusion.

When the old man makes a demand for money
in a whisper, the ventriloquist feeling in his
pockets assumes a disturbed expression and attitude, suggesting to the audience that he is annoyed
at such a subject being introduced, or such a request
being made during the performance and he says,

"You should not have asked me for money."

"Oh, all right, Guv'nor—if you ain't got any."

*(The Vent: then becomes indignant and sends
him away.)*

These effects are of course due to the acting,
the humour is not entirely Ventriloquial, were

it made so it would not be so funny, though it
would go to prove what I have said that Ventriloquism is not acting, but that *its effects are
enhanced by .acting*, as a well arranged accompaniment aids a song, though no one would
say that it was the song, because the song could
be given without it, but, like the acting to Ventriloquism, the accompaniment adds to the effect
of the song, and this is really how acting stands
in relation to Ventriloquism

Ventriloquial Vocabulary.

THE Vent: voice must be that of a coarse-speak-
ing person, and in imitating a man's voice it is
customary to suggest an Irishman, a yokel, or some
provincial dialect. You cannot Ventriloquize with
the woman's voice, nor with that of the little girl,
though you can with dogs, sheep, rooks, etc. In
"near" Ventriloquism the old woman's speech
must be common and even the child's, however
flexible the voice of the Ventriloquist, will not
be the voice of an aristocrat though it is the
least vulgar of all the voices.

It is a matter of congratulation that the man's
voice is the one that can be ventriloquized, because
supposing that it had been the woman's, and the
woman had to be on the roof, in the "cellar

cool," or out of doors, this unnatural arrangement
would have shown up the weakness of the art
and the limit of the voices.

It is impossible to imitate a " Fop" or " Swell"
in Ventriloquism, as you cannot aspirate an H,
and you must speak at the back of the mouth,
which is what the lower classes do, whereas the
aristocrat rather inclines to use the front of his
mouth, and the man who affects a super-refinement
of speech forces his words almost against his
front teeth in order to be thought refined, though
to nearly everyone, and especially to those who
mimic voices he only appears affected. A labourer
says, " 'Ow are you?" and his lips and tongue
hang loose. The swell says, " Howdy do?" and
screws up his upper lip and contracts his lower
till he could say " plum " very easily.

This strong distinction exists, and it is the
reason that in Ventriloquism in which sounds are
made at the *back of the* mouth—the only means
of making them distant—it is impossible to imitate
a " Fop " or " Swell ". or that style of speech
associated—not, of course, correctly in all cases—
with what is supposed to be an evidence of social
superiority. A negro in saying " what " will use
five notes from the back of the mouth but an
English gentleman becomes nasal and his "what!"

is short. As far as we are concerned the fact that the aristocracy are safe from Ventriloquial caricature may be accepted. If you like to try and give a Ventriloquial imitation of the Prince of Wales, I will give you his permission, because I know you will never succeed. This knowledge like similar information through this book tells you what cannot be done, which information I know would have saved me a lot of work, and if this book had been published before I wrote it I would be without those grey hairs I now perceive among my otherwise golden curls.

Having settled the limits of voices that can be used, we have to consider what words can be used most effectively and those which cannot be used at all.

If you wish to represent a man outside asking for beer—a request which in spite of the temperance movement and the new local option bil' is still recognized as characteristic—he must ask for a "*quart*" not a "*pint*", because without bringing the lips together you cannot say "*pint*", nor in fact any word beginning with "P" If you try you will say "'int" and can say nothing nearer with still lips.

It is obvious therefore that all words cannot be used, so we have "*possible dialogue.*" All

styles of speech cannot be imitated, so our illustrations become limited, not only to *certain styles
of speech* but even then with a *restricted vocabulary.*

When to use " possible dialogue " and when to
resort to artifice to conceal mouth-moving articulation has already been referred to under " Ventriloquial Acting ", what " possible dialogue " is
and what is " restricted " is what concerns us here.

I could write out a list of words and say
" use these"; but I do not believe in that style
of instruction, but prefer to give good general
advice, and my reasons for thinking I am right,
when I hope you will accept the advice and
think as I do, or possibly go a step higher and
improve upon my suggestions.

By telling you there is vocabulary that is
inadmissible in Ventriloquism, you are put on
your guard, and, instead of being disheartened
by failing to use successfully prohibited vocabulary, you understand that the fault may lie not in
yourself but in the dialogue, which you alter,
and discover that you have the key to all future
trouble of that kind. *To know whether words
are suitable, test them.*

If you are bidding your oral friend farewell
you say " good-night " and he says " good-night ";
though you perform at a matinee—" good-even-

ing", "good-afternoon," are not suitable salutations. "What do you say?" is a useful query.
As a precursor it arrests and secures attention for
your Ventriloquy, "Guv'nor" is a good title, "Sir"
a bad one; *you* use "Sir" and in Vent: "Guv'nor"
"I've got a ladder" is good, "ladder" is easily
made clear. "All right," "I'm 'ere, " "'E's down
below," "Keep yer 'air on", "'Ave yer got a
shilling?" are all useful. Long conversation in.
Ventriloquy is exhausting, and not so effective
as short remarks; your natural speech should, as
suggested before, take up most of the time.

Writing Vent: dialogue successfully is impossible without practical knowledge. There are men
who profess to supply it but they often send
recitations, and matter that is unsuitable. It is
the change from one voice to another, grotesque
noises, coughing, sneezing, etc., which allow no
time for criticism that amuse much more than
a sustained monologue which, however clever,
with Figures becomes wearisome. The recital of
"Three little mice", by the Little Girl is of little
effect unless broken up.

Illustration.

Vent:　　(*at screen*) "Ah! you are here,
　　　　Katy!"

Little Girl. "Yes, Mr. ——" (*the performer's name if pronounceable.*) "I've been 'ere all the evening."

Vent: "And now you are here, will you do something to amuse the company?"

L. G. "What's that?"

Vent: "Will you sing or recite?"

L. G. "I'll sing."

Vent: "That's right, you'll sing.

L. G. "Or recite."

Vent: "Yes or recite."

L. G. "Then I'll sing—may I stop here?"

Vent: "Eh!" (*head behind screen.*) "What is it?" (*whisper.*)

L. G. "I've got my second best socks on."

Vent: "Now then, Katy, sing."

L. G. "I said I was going to recite."

Vent: "Really, Katy, I don't know what you did say."

L. G. "That's why I tell you—
    "Three little mouses."

Vent: "Mice."

L. G. "Mouses—"

Vent: "Mice not mouses."

L. G. "Mice—"

Vent: "Ah!"

L. G. "What do you say 'ah' for? There

are no 'ahs.'   I must begin and commence all over again.

> " Three little mouse—"

Vent.   " Mice."

L. G.   " Is this your recitation or mine? If
you say anything more I shan't do it.

> " Three little mice sat down to spin

don't waggle your fingers," *(or any
other remark.)*

Vent: "I beg your pardon," *(stopping
movement.)*

L. G.
> " Three little mice sat down to spin,
> Pussey passed by and she—"

Vent: " Peeped in, yes."

L. G.   " It isn't 'peeped in yes.' Look here, am
I reciting this or are *you* reciting it? "

Vent: " You, of course."

L. G.   " Well, then, don't interrupt."

> " Pussey passed by and she peeped in
> What are you doing—

Vent: " I was not doing anything."

L. G.   " No, you ain't pussey, that's in the
piece—

> " What are you doing, my little men?
> Making coats for gentlemen.
> Shall I come in and bite off your threads
> Oh, no, Miss Puss, you'd bite off our heads.

and that's all of it, and am I to have
sixpence or a cheesecake?"

This sort of thing does not perhaps appear
amusing to read, but it will entertain an audience
better than clever wit, because to a certain extent
it is the natural behaviour of a precocious child caricatured, and the interruptions are humorous surprises.

Literary men on reading a Vent: Entertainment
would wonder why something better is not substituted, but it is *experience* that gives birth to
dialogues that really "go".

It in no wise follows that a clever novelist can
write a play that shall prove actable, a song that
is singable, minstrel sketch, Ventriloquial dialogue
etc., etc., for each requires special knowledge and
different treatment to produce their special effects.

In a play for instance we rely in a great
measure on situation.

Supposing that a lady were secretly visited by
the son of a former marriage which she had concealed from her present husband. The son, a
young man, is embracing his mother when the
husband surprises them. All the author would
make him say would be:

"Wife!"

And a stage effect or situation is gained. The
audience know what is passing in the mind of

each for the actors express that. A novelist treating the same subject would describe at length the feelings of each.

In Ventriloquism the acting never has this human interest for the personages are caricatures, and only afford laughter.

The literary merit of a song is secondary to its suitability to musical treatment.

What sounds very funny in a negro entertainment would sound very incongruous with white faces, and vice versa. Music Hall wit is justly ridiculed by those who give it attention but with drinking and smoking you do not get attention but an *inattentive** audience and broad obvious jokes, only succeed. Music Hall artists supply what their experience tells them is likely to succeed, writers write what their experience tells them is suitable, and it is with Ventriloquism you must use such dialogue as experience suggests. People do not look for great thoughts, well turned sentences and the grace of literary style in Ventrilo uism, for the Dialogue is subservient to

---

* In the best London Variety Entertainments the audience every day pay more attention to the stage, and when the clatter of programme girls and waiters' impromptu debating societies are a little restricted, we shall have a very delightful form of Entertainment and better class audiences.

the illustration of an art. I am compelled to digress a moment before I suggest any dialogue that is effective with Figures, otherwise you will be inclined to discard it.

I remember once as an amateur giving a Magic Lantern Entertainment at a workhouse. It was my first and last appearance in the capacity of Lantern worker. I had painted a number of artistic and humorous slides which I exhibited but they evoked no applause and little interest. In despair I thought I would try half a dozen hideous daubs that had been sent with the Lantern, and no sooner did I throw the first on the screen than the audience burst into applause, one inmate patronizingly remarking, "Aye, meister, that be more loike it."

Here is again an experience of "experience," and so it is with every branch of art.

The coarseness that Figures can utter with impunity and with effect, is remarkable. If you want to laugh you need only make the old man sneeze, and desire to borrow your handkerchief, cough, grunt, scream, imitate a cock crowing, tell his wife to "shut up," "wash her face" or "squint with her ears for a change" etc., etc.

During my noviciate I received a dialogue from "Professor" Bourne—to whom I am indebted for much sensible advice—which I discarded as being too outrageous, and wrote what I conceived to be better, with the same result as I have mentioned in the Magic Lantern Entertainment. My dialogue was received with respectful silence, but when I introduced his, which I had fortunately committed to memory, the house rose at it, and my debut as a Ventriloquist was a success.

Now I write my own, but I have experience now of the kind of thing that takes, and am successful in consequence. As in writing for the stage, don't use three words if the effect can be conveyed in one, Vent: dialogue must be brief and interruption should form a strong part of it.

Dialogue with old man, woman, and nigger.

Vent:	" Ladies and gentlemen—"
Old Man	" 'ear! 'ear! "
Vent:	" Silence, sir."
O. M.	" Only said 'Ear! 'ear! "
Vent:	" Ladies and gentlemen."
O. M.	*(sneeze)* " You said that afore "
Vent:	" Ladies and gentlemen—"
O. M.	" They know what they are without your telling 'em."
Vent:	" Silence! Ladies and—"
O. M.	*(sneezes)* gentlemen.
Vent:	" You have a cold "

O. M.	" Yes, got it 'ot "
Old Lady	" I knew he would "
O. M.	*(to O.L.)* " Don't you begin, you old scarecrow."
Vent:	" That's not the way to sp̣ ẹak to a lady, sir."
O. M.	" Er ain't a lady."
O. L.	" What am I then?"
O. M.	" My old gal—bless 'er 'art."
(sings)	" My old Dutch I likes to be near, and sing of 'er like Bertie Chevalier."
O. L. *(sings)*	" I cannot sing the old songs."
O. M.	' No, nor the noo 'uns either, so chuck it, old gal, chuck it."

Amalgamation of "near" and "distant".

THE difficulties of amalgamation are in the fusion and transition from one style of Ventriloquism to the other without exposing the " tricks of the trade " so to speak, without disclosing the art or disturbing the naturalness of the effect presented to the public.

The man that I have alluded to, who throws his voice to the ceiling and abruptly leaves it there with some lame excuse, is not a skilful amalgamator, but one-who some hat needlessly makes the art appear less comprehensive than it is in reality.

You will bring the man down from the roof because "he has a ladder," or you have the knowledge that enables him to dispense with one at the outlay of a little Ventriloquial perjury.

Having brought him to Level you further exhibit your ability by making him descend below and the change of position of voice must be covered by some "business," and it is always to me a pleasurable evidence of skill when I see a Ventriloquist make the change and score with the audience by the business he uses to cover such change.

The following dialogue shows an "amalgamation" in Ventriloquism without Figures, cf "Above" to "Below"

Vent:	"Jack!" *(pause)* "Jack!" *(it is as well to keep to one name for "above")*
Jack:	*("above")* "'Ullo!" *(prolonged as if shouting)*
Vent:	"Are you up there?"
Jack:	"All right, I'm 'ere."
Vent:	"Can you come down?"
Jack:	"All right! I got a ladder," *(sings)* "Tol de rol!"
Vent:	*(impatiently)* "Come along."

Jack: "All right, guv'nor—I aint a-going to break my neck—I'm getting lower down."

Vent: *(turning and looking up or away from audience)* "What's the matter?"

Jack: "There's a *spoke out*—or I wouldn't a *spoke out.*"

Vent: *(turning to audience with a disgusted expression)* "Bucolic wit!" *(to above)* "Come along."

Jack: "All right I'm coming, I'm a-coming one more and I'm 'ere."

Vent: "Where is here?" *(at door)*

Jack: ("*level distant.*") "No *where* ain't 'ere, *where* is *where* and 'ere is 'ere, and 'eres where you can 'ear me."

Vent: "You're witty."

Jack: "Yes, it's raining and I'm comin' in to dry myself."

Vent: "No, you mustn't come in."

Jack: "Oi says Oi must."

Vent: "No!"

Jack: "But Oi says yes."

Covering the action with his body Vent: partly opens door and as he does so changes his ventriloquism which he has used in Above to Level to near Grunt voice. From that moment he discards the Above and goes from Grunt to Below. Jack at the door arguing to come in, which you can of course extend as the dialogue is merely illustrative and must be altered to suit you.

Vent: "I say no," etc., etc.

Jack: "I says yes."

Vent: *(closing door)* "I say no."

Jack: *(distant as commencing "Level" to "Below")* "What do you want to shut the door in my face for?"

Vent: "You go down below, you'll find something there."

Jack: "Down these steps, guv'nor?"

Vent: "Yes."

Jack: "It's rather dark but I think I can manage—beer did you say? one two. *(lowering voice)* three, *(lower)* four. *(dog's bark heard)* Hullo, guv'nor. there's a dog down 'ere."

Vent: "Yes. I told you you'd find something."

This illustrates how by a little artifice you pass from one position of the vocal organs to another.

The assumption of deafness already alluded to can be often utilized in passing the voice from above.

Vent: "Jack!"

Jack: "What do you say?"

Vent: "Are you down?"

Jack: "I'm 'ere."

Vent: "I said are you down?"

Jack: "What do you say?"

Vent: "Don't say what do you say"

Jack: "All right, guv'nor, I won't say 'what do you say' if you don't want me to say 'what do you say' when I says 'what do you say.'"

During the laughter this fooling provokes you

Fig. 6.

change to, "Below" voice and down he goes.
I might mention here incidentally that when you
call, and you are not satisfied that the audience
are sufficiently attentive, or somebody is fid-
getting about, coming in late, or otherwise assist-
ing you, Jack becomes very deaf and cannot hear
anything until you think your Ventriloquism can
be heard.

In making the change when the door is partly
opened and your back is to the audience your
lips have full play and as your Ventriloquism
"Level and Near" requires little effort you can
have a tremendous row at the door, even to slipping
the arm out of your left coat sleeve if the door be
on the left and accompany your Ventriloquism by
a clever optical illusion.

EXPLANATION.

By simulating a struggle Vent: pushes Jack out,
takes the opportunity of slipping arm into coat
while stamping and talking, and returning into
room slams door and imitates Jack with "Distant
Level."

In arranging these effects try and obtain the
assistance of a friend to stage manage, as his
eye and ear will tell you what is effective and
what is not.

I have seen Dr. Broadbridge do this without Ventriloquism after a similar effect that I do of an imitation of two men wrestling. He came in, after he had disappeared fighting, with his handkerchief to his eye, which when asked he explained was the result of a blow the other fellow had given him. As Dr. Broadbridge is happily only an amateur conjuror though as clever as any professional before the public, he will probably not object to your copying his business of the damaged optic.

I am aware that the visible struggle is not Ventriloquism, but it is amazingly funny as is also my generosity in giving you permission to use what is distinctly my friend's property.

In amalgamatory Ventriloquism with "near" in using Figures they can be left and an entertainment of Ventriloquism given in the ordinary way without Figures. This shows too plainly that Figure working is a different art to Ventriloquism.

If on the other hand the "old man" suggests that the Vent: should do something, it comes about more naturally, and he can then Ventriloquize while working the Figures and improve the effect by interpolating their remarks.

ILLUSTRATION.

O. M.   "Now, guv'nor, you do something."

Vent: "I do something?"

O. M.   "Yes, you make us do the whole show and not so much as a glass of beer ever passes my lips."

C. L.   "You never pass a glass of beer you mean. Wah!" (*to O. M.*)

O. M.   "Wah!" (*to O. L.*)

The above two exclamations do not read as high-class wit, but a wrangle of this kind succeeds beyond belief in pleasing the audience.

Vent: "Silence!"

O. L.   (*Sneezes*)

O. M.   (*Sneezes*)

Vent: "Will you behave, sir."

O. M.   "Caught it from my old dutch (*sings*) it's a dutch cheese—I mean sneeze. Tol the rol lol!"

Vent: (*covers hand over O. M.'s mouth*)

O. M.   (*sings ventriloquially*). "Tol the rol lol, 'ere I can't breathe" (*Vent removes hand—O. M. loud voice*) Oh! Oh! you?—(*sneeze, sneeze, sneeze.*)

O. L.   "What do you think you are—a steam engine?"

O. M.	" Oh lor, he nearly smothered me."
Vent:	" Why don't you behave yourself then ? "
O. L.	" He don't know how."
O. M.	" Ditto, you old scarecrow."
Vent:	" That is not the way to address a lady."
O. M.	" She ain't a lady."
O. L.	" What am I then? "
O. M.	" My old girl, that's what you are, and now, 'guv'nor, go on with your show."
Vent:	" I suppose you know, sir, that I have a man on the roof."
O. M.	" I pity him a night like this."
Vent:	" I will call to him. Jack! "
O. M.	" You must call louder nor that."
Vent:	" Jack."
O. M.	*(very loud)* " Jack."
Vent:	" Jack."
O. L.	" Jack."
O. M.	" Jack! Jack! Jack! "
Vent:	*(above voice)* " Hullo"
O. M.	" I fetched 'im."
Vent:	" What are you doing up there? "
O. M.	" What's that got to do with you? "
Vent:	*(strikes him)*

O. M.	(*Crying*) Boo—boo—oh, oh!
Vent:	(*stuffs handkerchief into mouth: as he does so, cries become fainter and fainter till they cease and head is allowed to drop down on shoulder.*)

Here we have an amalgamation of Figure working and Ventriloquism which can be extended indefinitely. I might here add that supposing a Vent: dog were an added Figure you could bring in vocal mimicry; by carrying it off as it barked you could imitate it retreating into the distance by Ventriloquism. A bluebottle could buzz round the old man and much fun would be caused by your trying to kill it and hitting him every time until you squash the insect on his forehead.

In an amalgamated entertainment you can introduce anything you like, cork drawing, sawing wood, cock crowing, etc., by allowing the O. M. to provoke such illustrations.

O. M.	"I say can you crow like a cock?"
Vent:	"Yes, sir."
O. M.	"So can I."
Vent:	"I should be delighted to hear you."
O. M.	"You've never heard me?"
Vent:	"No."
O. M.	"I thought not or you wouldn't say that. Heres mine! (*crows*)"

Vent: (*Crows*)

O. M.   (*Crows etc.*)

Vent: "When are you going to stop?"

O. M.   "Not afore you does." (*crows*)

It is effective to introduce the Figure of a little girl from behind screen and do half the show with the figure seated on your knee.

Whatever Figure or whatever voice imitation you find you do best, introduce it most prominently but don't make the mistake of over doing it.

Illustrations in the dark can of course be done in conjunction with Dolls, or any form of amalgamation.

Dark Room Seance.

THIS is best introduced to show that Ventriloquism is not acting, nor really depending upon it, and is best introduced after a few illustrations in the light that do not discount what you intend to do in the dark, which should be the man above descending to the cellar, and as you must ventriloquize well in the dark to carry your point this must not be attempted until you are proficient, until you can make your voice appear *right away from you and in the room above or on the roof.* When it is dark the whole atten-

tion of the audience is with its ears, and therefore your success or failure is intensified, and if
you don't convince them that the voice can be
" thrown " you look ridiculous and had best decamp
before the lights are turned up again.

There are advantages in ventriloquizing in the
dark as well as drawbacks, for instance, though
you obtain no aid from acting, you are not
obliged to keep your lips still, you may speak
right at the ceiling with your head back, and
to the floor with your head down, which privileges materially assist you in obtaining your
effects and which privileges you keep to yourself. In the dark if you have dancing shoes on,
and can move without noise, the ghostly voice
is effective spoken say to your right, and then as
you sharply turn to your left; a struggle with
the man with the ghostly voice is amusing if
well rendered, it suggests the midnight assassin
and as the audience cannot see anyone they are
led to believe there are two.

You can pay money, pour out liquids in the
dark, and, if you have unlimited assurance, you
can pass the sound of the actual thing for vocal
mimicry. I do not suggest this for the paying
public as it would be dishonest, but among friends
a clever bit of humbug is, I think, permissible.

There are a variety of little comedies that can be acted in the dark, two men sleeping in a double-bedded room, one man who can't find the candle and when he does, matches don't strike (as you carefully use the wrong end), woman's voice at door saying there is a mistake and he is in the wrong room etc., etc.

Try any experiments on your own family and if they say "It is not so bad" you may be assured that it will delight strangers.

I might add that in a darkened room no change of scenery is required as this is suggested by the dialogue and whether you want a bed room or a wood you have it with a few words.

Optical Assistants.

WHERE figures are not used all sorts of expedients are resorted to to make the effect you produce appear possible to the eye, which makes the unaided Ventriloquism more difficult than where such forcible optical assistants are employed as mouth moving automata.

It would be sufficiently illusory to carry on a conversation with a little girl, on the opposite side of a cottage piano to the audience, as she would not be seen if she were there, but it would be absurd to do so with a man, as, unless he knelt, his head would appear over the top of piano.

Optical assistants and their efficacy is a thing apart from Ventriloquism, but, like acting, is an assistant.

If you are called upon to Ventriloquize when out walking, you do not immediately "throw your voice but gain time by assumed diffidence or conversational expedient, until you come to some suitable surrounding a grating, bush, wooden shed, etc., and then illustrate with suitable dialogue.

If it were possible for a man to be invisible and fly over your head, and you made *him* speak when asked to Ventriloquize on a moor your friend would have no interest in the illustration. it would be so obviously unnatural, as he would not be competent to judge what a voice really spoken in mid air sounded like : but if you knocked at a wooden shed and imitated a dog, the effect of having roused a dog would be familiar and therefore recognized and appreciated. You can throw your voice up in the open air, but, as I said, there is no excuse, no meaning in it, so the effect goes for nothing. In a fog you might call to a wall and carry on a conversation with men at the top, or in an imaginary balloon for that matter, if the fog prevented your seeing it, up a tree if in full leaf etc., or as long as something, no matter whether fog, leaves, screen or piano intervenes to prevent the eye contradicting the evidence of the ear.

I have seen an otherwise good Ventriloquial effort spoilt because the performer had not allowed sufficient cover for the people his Ventriloquy suggested.

There is a vast difference in the suitability of rooms. Some offer admirable opportunities for effect: others make Ventriloquism without Figures almost impossible.

Rich draperies kill the sounds as they do in singing, the position of the doors, windows, etc., the irregular seating of your audience and their proximity make Drawing-Room Ventriloquism very difficult and more of an improvised character as the dialogue and business must be altered to a great extent to suit each particular room you visit.

It will often be noticed that singers and actors who are most successful on the platform or stage disappoint when heard in a room, this is often due to their surroundings and I consider this more true of Ventriloquism than of anything else.

If you employ such optical assistants as Figures and work them with "near" Ventriloquism you are more independent of surroundings, a set dialogue can be gone through parrot-like which lasts a certain time and your show is finished.

Figures that do well for the stage are needlessly hideous when as near as they would be in a drawing-room and dialogue that is quite strong enough for a room would appear weak over the footlights, and what is toned down by the distance of a theatre or hall in dialogue would be offensive in a room.

It is possible to use much broader humour through Figures than would be tolerated in the ordinary way, for they, like dwarfs, are privileged persons, though I don't see why they should be. This remark is pertinent here in reference to the employment of Figures as assistant surroundings.

The Ventriloquist should act as a mediator between the Figures and the audience, correcting their vagaries, and showing uneasiness at their want of breeding. This serves to convey the idea that they are different creatures with different ideas, education, etc.

I remember one young man—who has given up touting for coal orders to amuse the upper circles—giving a Ventriloquial exhibition during which he turned to the old man in propriâ persona and exclaimed "You shut up" and "none of your jaw." This repugnant and inartistic style of

work, it will scarcely be conceived, appeals to the
level of the critical acumen of the representatives
of certain West End Agencies, and the perpetrator
of it is sent out to lower the taste of society
whenever opportunity occurs.

There is nothing more suitable than a stage
upon which to give an entertainment, the wall
of warm air from gas footlights has a separative
quality and the proscenium cuts off sound and
disperses it into the Flies and gives it a distant
effect, provided of course that you do not come
down until your face is almost over the footlights,
as singers do who wish to appear to have turned
up noses.

The effect of sounds, the difficulty the audience
have of localizing their origin is so well understood, by those who study stage effect, that should
an actress be required to sing who cannot, she
has only to simulate singing, when the song supplied by a vocalist at the wings will appear to
be hers, without any fear of the audience being
able to detect the dual nature of the performance.
Unlimited impudence I have seen substituted for
Ventriloquism by men who discover the liberties
that can be taken on the stage with impunity; as
an illustration of *voice throwing* I have seen an
Entertainer place a head on one side of the stage

and then inform the audience that he would "throw his voice across the stage" whereupon he used "near," with still lips, and by pulling the string moved the mouth and created the illusion that the actress and the vocalist created, though they did not call it voice throwing.

My motive in alluding to this is to demonstrate the assistance offered by the stage as it may be useful to you and, moreover, you will, while enjoying any illusion of the kind, accept "cum grano salis" any statements made over the footlights by those who sacrifice truth to gain credit for powers they do not possess. They will be found out with the progress of knowledge, if the classics of our school days are correct which says "Magna est veritas, et prevalebit."

If you try the experiment of making a head talk across the stage and introduce the illustration by saying "I will make the head appear to talk" the effect is equally interesting and you avoid misleading falsehood. If the public say that you throw your voice that is their affair.

When a greater distance is phonetically suggested on the stage or a voice is heard through an intervening roof or floor then you employ Ventriloquism and must throw the voice, or no effect is created as the eye is not humbugged by

6

a - mouth-moving head. This is the distinction between near and Vent:, and, supposing that the public knew as much about Ventriloquism as we do, it would not injure the art but make it more appreciated.

As the difficulty of localizing sounds is part of phonetics I might by way of illustration recall the difficulty we have in finding friends in a wood, and how often the calling must be repeated to discover each others whereabouts.

It is the same in the house, even while I write I hear an example, my wife calls a servant.

"Mary."

"Yes, marm."

"*Where are you?*"

The girl has answered, and yet it is difficult to be certain whether she is upstairs or down, or at all events to be certain exactly where she is.

When close it is much easier to localize a sound, though even in a room the sound of a mouse not being loud its whereabouts are not ascertained without repeated listening; the principle is the same, regulated by the proportions of sound to space, whether it be a mouse nibbling paper in the room or the explosion of a distant powder mill. In both cases the listener is not quite certain of the exact locality and when an

explosion takes place it is, generally surmised to
be a neighbouring "Gas work" or "powder
magazine" because such things offer the most
probable solution. When the Regent Canal explosion took place resulting from explosives in
a barge, a man who had the side of his house
blown out flew like a madman along the streets
shouting " *The Zoological Gardens have blown up.*"
This may be taken as an example of the difficulty of locating sound and the readiness with
which people, fix the source of sound on the first
place that comes to their minds.

The nearer the sound the greater force of
proportion it bears to the radius of which you—
the hearer—are the centre. At three yards sound
is more easily located than at three miles, and
three miles at three miles would less easily be
located than three feet at three yards, so that the
stage or platform makes phonetic deceit more
easy than it would be when performed at close
quarters in a room.

I am often asked if I can throw my voice to
the roof of a large building? The questioner
forgetting that ventriloquial speech is in inverse
ratio to ordinary speech and that to throw the
voice, the greater the distance the *fainter* the
speech not the *louder.*

In a Ventriloquial sketch that I have given to thousands of people in all parts of the country I imitate a phonograph, my first " Record" being a Scotch gentleman playing a Scotch bagpipe on a Scotch mountain twenty Scotch miles distant.

After keeping the audience listening for some time no sound is recorded which, as I explain, "*shows the accuracy of the apparatus.*"

Provided therefore that the sound is sufficiently distant to be inaudible anyone can imitate it.

Special Optical Assistants

BY these I mean talking hands, heads, Vent: Figures for which special dialogue can be arranged, which makes the performer independent of local surroundings as far as optical assistants and impromptu speech are concerned.

Some performers find it absolutely necessary to have everything they say or do arranged beforehand, while some find that they can rely upon impromptu gags to supplement a sparse dialogue. To the former the Figures are almost a requisite as the business and dialogue can be alike adhered to, whereas the man of spontaneous wit and a ready adaptability to local surroundings, gains by what I have termed ordinary optical assistants, as his resource is shown by this form of Entertainment just as much as the want of resource is concealed by the employment of Figures.

One acrobat performs on a "slack wire" another on a "tight rope" because, although they could both do either, one form of gymnastics suits each individual best, and so it is with the particular method of exploiting Ventriloquy.

In using Figures an audience know perfectly well that they do not speak, but they lend themselves to the illusion for the amusement it affords them.

Figure Working

THERE is a right and a wrong way in working a set of figures and unless the Entertainer has imagination and uses it to make the audience believe that his Figures do talk, the Entertainment loses half its charm.

I have seen a Ventriloquist come on to a stage drag off the covers from a couple of Figures, announce that he had the honour to give the audience a Ventriloquial Entertainment and then go straight through a set dialogue, bow, and retire.

The very last thing an artist would do, would be to inform the audience that he was going to give a Ventriloquial Entertainment. He *is* going to *do* that so he does not talk about it. ' Any introduction is better than that, though it is a very common one, so much so as to be hackneyed, which is another reason for avoiding it.

On entering bow to the audience, and commence:—"Ladies and gentlemen,"—and then, seeing old man, say, as you shake his hand,

> *Vent:* "Oh, you're here already, are you?"
>
> *O. M.* "Yes, came down in the luggage van, haven't 'ad nothing to eat since breakfast (*coughs.*)
>
> *Vent:* "You have caught cold?"
>
> *O. M.* "Yes, plenty of it in that luggage van" (*coughs.*)"
>
> *O. L.* "What's that—a dog barking."
>
> *Vent:* "No, your husband."
>
> *O. L.* "And where's Katy?" ("*Toby*", *dog, Pussey, etc.*)

This dialogue illustrates an informal introduction. You may come on, bow and go to the old man and pull him about working his head so as to watch you.

> *O. M.* "What's up, guv'nor."
>
> *Vent:* (*business.*)
>
> *O M.* "If the string's broke I may as well go home."

Vent:	"How dare you speak about strings, showing me up before the public, exposing the art by which—"
O. M.	"Oh, chuck it, guv'nor, chuck it."
O. L.	"What's the matter with yer string?
O. M.	"Nothing—new last Wednesday."
Vent:	"Silence!"
O. M.	(*sings*) "For the British Grenadier Hip, hip hurrah!"
Vent:	"If you say that again I'll—"
O. M.	"Hip hip" (*Vent: raises his hand to strike him*) "Hipecaquanha lozenges."
Vent:	(*Drops hand*)
O. M.	(*To audience*) "Got him on the cough drop."

Be very careful not to look at a Figure when it is about to address you. I don't mean by that always look away from it, but there is natural tendency to look where your thoughts are and to the Figure you know is about to speak. Supposing the Figures were alive their thoughts would be unknown to you, and it would not be until those thoughts were put into words, and those words addressed to you, that you would hear them and turn to the speaker.

In Figure working you are sustaining an illusion and the more you trick the audience against their better judgment into believing that the Figures speak, the more successful you will be.

If you are whispering to the O.L. and you make the O.M. keep looking round, shake his head and express disgust and while your lips are close to O.L., he says, while the back of your head is to him, "Stop that, guv'nor, no kissing my old woman."

The effect is as though he had become jealous and remonstrated on his own account. This effect without being overdone can be worked in various ways to the bewilderment of the judgment of the audience.

Anything unforeseen that happens during the

Entertainment should be taken advantage of and commented upon. In this a Vent: Figure entertainment has an enormous advantage over others, as interruptions do not interrupt but assist, as the show itself is nothing but interruptions.

If an old gentleman in the audience drops his umbrella, or knocks over a chair, the Vent: immediately stops his "set dialogue" and gets what he can out of the accident in some such dialogue as the following.

> O. M.   "I say, guv'nor, that gent's broke one of the 'all chairs."
>
> *Vent:*   "Silence!"
>
> O. M.   "Yes—and then you'll dock it out of my salary."
>
> O. L.   "He's picking it up now."
>
> *Vent:*   "Will you go on with the Entertainment?"
>
> O. M.   "Not while the brokers—I mean the breakers are in—"

People entering, windows being opened or shut, all interrupt and make it difficult for an ordinary performer to go on, but the Vent: does not suffer provided he makes capital out of unforeseen interruptions, which, if cleverly availed of, give a life-like effect to the Figures as they appear to hear, see, think and speak.

Mr. Maskelyne makes an interesting blunder—the blunder a show man would, but an artist would never make—and I introduce it as an antithetical illustration of the simulated hearing of the Ventriloquial Figure.

He exhibits a sketching automaton made on the principal of the well known pantograph. Having by elaborated talk and demonstration shown the Figure to be in no way connected with a human director, he says to it, "Are you ready?" *

The Figure bows in response, _and at once reveals the presence of a human agency directing its movements which he was at such pains to conceal._

The Ventriloquist makes his Figures appear to hear by hearing for them and that quality which a Vent: Figure should possess is a fatal quality to an automaton, whose speciality its exhibitor assures the public is in its being entirely mechanical.

If you intend imitating instruments, animals, other than those of which you use models, make such imitations through the Figures, they always go better, and your Figures are not left out in the cold.

* "_Rise_ your arm." was the exact phrase until this grammatical inelegance was corrected by a man in the Gallery.

Songs of a kind give variety **to an** Entertainment and a chorus can, often introduce one
voice after the other which makes an effective
finish to a show.

An amusing change is caused by making the
O. M. or O. L. whisper by simply moving their
mouths in silence.

The old man can bite the Vent:'s finger with
ood effect, should it wander too near his mouth,
and numberless other bits of business will suggest
themselves in the course of practice and performance.

VOCAL MIMICRY.

THIS is the imitation of sounds other than of speech, and it only becomes Ventriloquism when the distant sound of such mimicry is produced. For instance a boy imitates a dog barking which is "mimicry;" if he transfer that sound to a distance he must first place the vocal organs in position for Ventriloquy and so he employs Ventriloquism or Ventriloquial mimicry.

It is not possible to give a distant imitation, of *all* the various things that can be mimicked by the voice, the general run of sounds cannot be Ventriloquized nor would it be a natural imitation if they could.

What can be imitated by the human voice is sufficiently extraordinary, and as the different ways of imitating the same sounds are numerous, the best method only I shall point out to you.

In vocal mimicry unless you are employing

animal automata or optical assistants you can move
the lips, in fact in what are termed " Farmyard"
imitations the cock bird's actions are elaborately
caricatured by the performer, the fidelity of the
strut, the flapping of wings prior to the crow,
the stretching of the neck are all imitated. This
of course would be ridiculous in illustrating distant
sounds. You can bring in a canvas covered coop,
crow near for the bird inside, repeating his general
challenge Ventriloquially or pretend the bird first
heard is at the side wings, behind a door, etc.,
or personate it yourself. The effect of the canvas
covered coop is not to make the crow *remote*,
but give an excuse for its origin and sustain the
illusion.

Cock crowing

ANYONE can crow like a cock if he imitate
nature. But there are as many varieties of crowing as of spiders. The shrill little Bantam, the
awkward bungling crow of the Asiatic breeds
such as the Brahma or Cochin, the clarion note
of the Game or Black Spanish, the peculiarity
of the Houdan and the laughable attempts of the
young cockerels when learning. All are effective
in contrast against each other. I doubt if most
people know the different crows of different

breeds, but they would be interested to learn if you gave them examples of each kind. If you imitate a Bantam's crow use the "punch" voice, and you will get it at once. For other kinds you *partly assume Ventriloquial attitude as regards the chest.* People as a rule hear a cock crow at a distance—not in a room—so that if you are performing in a room, a slightly Ventriloquial effect is the most truthful. After the studies you have done I feel certain you will understand this suggestion without difficulty, when your ear will inform you what is correct.

Ducks.

IN imitating ducks you must not say "quack because a duck, having no lips, does *not* say quack. I think a duck tries to say quack, and if you try and say 'uack and do not use your lips, but use your mouth as a duck does its upper and lower bill, opening it as wide as you can and making the exaggerated action the bird does, you will hear from your mouth an exact imitation of its cry. The first "'uack" must be loud and the following "'uacks" quick and fainter. At the cost of a bit of loaf and a visit to a duck pond, a few ducks will give you finishing lessons as long as the bread lasts.

Parrot.

As a rule people suggest for this bird's articulation the most difficult words possible "Pretty Polly," no parrot ever said, or ever will say "Pretty Polly" * for the same reason a duck does not say "quack." For a parrot and for parrot-talk you use the "punch" voice, but you must avoid labials, or if you do your imitation is recognized as that of a "human" as the American calls him, imitating a parrot. If you listen very carefully to the bird you'll perceive that what I say is correct, and by giving your attention to these small matters your imitation becomes similar to nature and therefore deceives.

By going to a cage, no one could tell it was not the parrot speaking, if you give the mimicry with boldness, and with human speech show the defects of the bird when using it.

Cat

I AM sorry to refute so many household beliefs but the cat does not *me*—iow but *e*—iow and this is also as capable, or more capable of proof than the absent labial of the parrot or duck—at least it is in my neighbourhood any fine evening after dark. The study of cat dialogue, moreover, is cheaper than that of duck's, as no bread is

*A parrot says " 'itty '-olly."

necessary to encourage them to give illustrations of their vocalism.

Bluebottle.

ONE of the easiest imitations, and one that is always a success is that of a bluebottle flying about the room, which you try and catch. There are many things about this performance which makes it effective. As for instance when you pretend to follow it, you naturally take the sound with you, which is the same thing in effect as if the insect made the buzzing and you followed that. You are permitted by virtue of your employment to turn your back to the audience. When you want to take breath the imaginary bluebottle has a polite habit of resting on the curtains or on the wall. Having gained your breath you start the insect again by a flip of your handkerchief and so on until you smash it, or capture it. Let it buzz in your hand, throw it down and explode it with a stamp of your foot, and give it with a little judicious imitation, its coup de grace.

The bluebottle is made by blowing through the lips until they vibrate rapidly while you are uttering a droning sound—*not the Ventriloquial Drone*—but a near moan about the pitch of the hum of a bluebottle. That the insect has its characteristic tone was distinctively proved by the clever imitation of a bluebottle by the 'cello (alternating B, B flat and A or similar half tones) during the pantomimic acting of pierrot fils catching one in "L'Enfant Prodigue." The vibration of the wings in the vocal imitation is represented by the vibration of the lips, which disturb the air in a similar manner to the 'cello and the insect and with the added moan give a realistic though rather exaggerated imitation of a bluebottle. This mimicry is a very powerful one when acquired completely, and is very effective in large Halls or Theatres where the Ventriloquial or distant bee could not be heard.

You will make a good deal of spluttering in your first attempt at getting that near hum of the bluebottle, and its attainment will be accelerated or retarded according to the formation of your lips, but if you have lips you can succeed, and if you do flounder about in practising you may, for you cannot do yourself any hurt in learning a labial accomplishment of this kind.

Circular Saw Mill.

THE reason I follow the bluebottle by a saw mill is because in mimicry they should be in sequence, the revolving hum of **the saw being,** in effect, a grossly exaggerated bluebottle. By protruding the lips, closing them and blowing through them *without making any vocal sound* you will soon be reminded of a saw mill in full operation. The difference of tones made from the initial incision of the saw into the timber, to its exit can all be simulated by slightly altering the position

Fig. 8. of the lips. As the teeth of the saw cut more slowly, you exhale more slowly, and by using more breath, you get that regular hum, which has been attained before in distant Vent:, which is in principal the shake in singing that commences by slowly alternating two notes and finally increases until you obtain the sustained shake.

Donkey.

THE preliminary squeak to the bray of the ass is made by the animal drawing in its breath sharply. You can imitate this in the same way, but it is less hurtful to the voice to use the "punch" voice first for what I have designated the preliminary squeak, doing the whole imitation while exhaling.

will stand
tinue his

Water.

THE turning on of a tap, and the first burst
of compressed air is suggested by "pfitt", and the
sound of water coming into a cistern or pail by
the use of more saliva. The cistern experiment
is best as so many people have had occasion to
listen to these sounds, and so they are familiar
with them and they recognize the imitation.

Tearing Calico.

THIS is made by fixing the off lip and risible
muscles in the position they would be if you
grinned, when you close them and draw the air
into the mouth opposite the molar teeth, the
effect of tearing calico is imitated exactly.

Squeaking door or gate.

THIS comes at once to anyone familiar with the
"punch" voice.

I remember once, when I was more reckless
than I am now, imitating the squeak of the
garden gate as I opened it to my hostess. I
concluded she didn't appreciate my humour, so
attempted no more. Next day I saw the servant
hard at work on the hinges of the innocent gate
with the salad oil bottle acting under orders. I
explained my joke and ever since I have been

given sardines, additional oil in my salad, etc., in order to prevent the gate from squeaking again.

MUSICAL INSTRUMENTS.

THE imitation of musical instruments has recently obtained a higher state of excellence than was thought of some time ago. As a rule such imitations being imitations become tiresome, as any imitation always will if continued too long. Mr. Atkinson's imitations of the mandoline, are the best I have heard, but when he follows mandoline with a banjo played as mandoline or other similar effect he over-rates the avidity of the audience for one dish in his Entertainment menu. My idea has always been to combine vocal instrumentation with a song, letting it form part of the song. I have for years made a specialty of songs of this kind, some of which are published by Messrs. Reynolds and Co., 13 Berners Street, London, and the large sale they now command is an evidence of public appreciation of this combination which no doubt will create numerous songs that embody the same idea.

The advantage of the imitation in the song is that it is not too long to tire the listener, and not beyond the capacity of the performer, as a long imitation solo might be.

Banjo.

IN imitating the Banjo you say "Pang" in the same fashion as you say "'uack" for the duck with this difference that the P is articulated. If instead of "Pang" you say "Tang" you can use your tongue more and give the sound of the old fashioned roll by saying "Trrr-ang." As a matter of fact "Pang" and "Tang" are both correct, if the Banjo be listened to the two sounds will be heard as the strings are struck in different ways. I am refering to the old fashioned Banjo for it is as well to avoid imitations that take and keep the voice on high notes. "Prr-ang tang" would give the sound of the thumb rubbed across the strings followed by a single note picked out with the forefinger. When I say that "Pang" and "Tang" are correct I mean that they approximate as nearly in sound as any written word I can use, and form the basis of practice while you copy the instrument when played. "Sambo's Serenade" introduces the Banjo in a manner that is not difficult and yet effective. I have never found this song fail to make a good impression so I can recommend it in connection with this imitation, with the certainty that it will be liked. This song, if you have an accompanist can be amusingly rendered by your taking an umbrella—tuning it, etc., by mimicry and then using it as a Banjo when you do the imitation. In addition to the pianoforte there is a special Banjo accompaniment and if you have a Banjo, as well as a piano the effect is most amusing.

You might imagine that the real Banjo would destroy your imitation, but it does not for though the audience might possibly perceive that yours was an imitation if alone, when they hear the Banjo as well, the quality you fail to give is supplied and the effect is that of a couple of Banjos playing together.

Xylophone.

THIS instrument is also known by the more suggestive title of pine sticks, as it consists of a number of pieces of wood of different lengths which on being struck with a hammer give out different notes of a hollow quality. It would be imagined that such a sound would be impossible to repeat vocally and yet I have by practice become able to give Scotch airs and variations to the accompaniment of a full orchestra.

Fix your mouth in position by saying " oh." Then take your open hands and hold them so that the right thumb comes a little below the left, which if you hollow the hand slightly leaves a triangular opening above the latter. By separating the hands, and then bringing them sharply together the collected air between the palms is forced with percussion through the triangular opening, which being brought opposite the opening formed by the lips when saying " oh " you obtain a note. You will soon discover after a few experiments that by making the opening of your lips *smaller* the *notes become lower* by making it *larger* the *notes become higher.*

I introduced this in a song called the " Xylophone" and it was singularly taking, but I must mention that after practising this imitation my lips became so swollen that their size was a disfigurement, and, though my Doctor was inclined to doubt my theory about the Xylophone practice being the cause, I attributed the swelling to the continual percussive stream of cold air sent against the lips. The time devoted to practice anything of this kind is not comprehensible to outsiders. I may be wrong in my surmise against medical opinion, but in telling you how to imitate pine sticks I think it right to give you my experience, and leave you to act as you please. One thing I found necessary in my Xylophone studies was to bandage my eyes, as the stream of air occasionally went into them and caused them to become bloodshot just as though I had been in the draught from a cab or railway carriage window.

Trombone.

THIS imitation is a labial one that almost every-one can do, and if the performer have an ear for music and imitates a solo to a piano accompaniment it is amusing, but the weakness of this imitation lies in the strength of the instrument imitated, which is its chief characteristic, and which is absent in the imitation.

Cornet.

THIS should *not* be attempted with the *lips*, but made at the top of the palate "Ta-ta-ta"; the reality of which is increased by holding the hand half clenched and making the sound through it.

This style of imitation, though of course faint in comparison to the instrument imitated, is very effective even in large Halls. It is really the "theek" of the "punch" pronounced "ta" instead of "theek" which knowledge will enable you to master production without difficulty. By the use of saliva you produce the burr that often precedes the clear blown note, the faulty production arising

from water in the cornet or some of the many
tricks with which wind instruments continually
surprise the player. These defects are less in
evidence with our best players who, by constant
care, avoid them, but they are never entirely
absent from any performance on a wind instrument
when the *note must be made*, and not, as in a piano
where it is already made for you. For purposes
of humorous imitation a cornet player at a street
corner who has been copiously supplied with
drink by a neighbouring publican is the most
likely model to supply points of characterization,
which, though objectionable to hear in a solo,
are amusing in an imitation because in the
latter they evidence observation, and mimicry.
The late Mr. Fred Leslie gave an admirable
travesty of a cornet, suggesting the keys with
the fingers of the left hand which he played on
with his right using the aperture of the partially
closed left hand to focus the sound he made
and to which I have before alluded. He imitated
the blowing through the cornet to clear it, turning it upside down, flipping the keys to see if
they worked properly, etc., etc. All of which is
mimetic, but purely that mimicry of the actor
which appeals to the eye, or speaking broadly it
is "Ventriloquial Acting." If Mr. Leslie had not

found his preliminary introduction effective he would have discarded it, as no Entertainer can sacrifice the reputation he has made, or the reputation he hopes to make, by doing anything that causes him to lose favour with the public. So that when I say he elaborated his cornet imitation, as I have described, it means that you can do it with advantage if you desire.

Musette.

A FAINT imitation of this instrument is given by a method that does not exactly recommend itself to those who entertain in Drawing-Rooms. You pinch your nose with your fingers and saying " ta " use the " theek " or " punch " voice which you will find materially changed in character by the stoppage of the nostrils. With an instrument that is so constructed that each note, as in a penny whistle, has a separate hole, or is made by a stoppage of certain holes, gliding is impossible except so far as a half tone is made by lifting the finger *gradually* off the hole. Yet I have heard a gentleman glide while imitating a musette, as though it were a violin, which is incorrect though some people will be found to exclaim when they hear it " How like a musette!" though they never heard one in their lives before, which may have been in a measure, their reason for eulogistical criticism. A pair of pince nez made to order would hold the nose politely I should think.

Italian pipe.

THIS is a reed instrument of primitive construction used by the Savoyard peasant. It is higher than the clarinette though there is a resemblance in the top notes of the latter to the ordinary register of the other. You place the tongue against the palate and using "punch" say "te" prolonging the note and giving a turn to the tip of the tongue as you pass from one note to another, perhaps if you say " Te-del-le " you will understand me.

I remember in studying art, a well-known Academecian said to me when I was painting the complexion of a face "think of a peach—not a brick wall " and just in the same way when you imitate the Italian pipe think of one. If you have never heard one you cannot imitate it correctly, and if you find it difficult to hear one, take a similar character of instrument in more general use and imitate that.

Clarinette.

The music in the streets has improved with the general advance of culture in England, and the retelically coloured clarionet, with sciatica in its lower joints, is unfortunately, for purposes of humorous imitation, as extinct in our streets now as the Dinotherium or Megalosaurus. Occasionally an old man is seen wandering along the gutter with a clarionet, and in proportion to his destitution will he enrich the music of our best composers with twirls and shakes. I remember one old man whose twirls almost, but not quite, obliterated the original melody, which when nearly lost was suddenly reverted to in vigorous blasts, only to be again dissipated in a series of interminable twirls. In imitation this sound should be practised "tul-le" at the lower back of mouth making the sound towards the top as the higher notes are produced. There is a lot of character in a badly played clarinette and if you could introduce a friend to learn one it would be an advantage to you provided he did not reside in a neighbourhood where you possessed property.

Bass fiddle.

As to obtain higher sounds than are possible from a 'cello we use the viola, and the violin, each smaller and consequently using shorter strings, so to obtain deeper sounds we use larger models made with longer strings, such as the Bass fiddle and still lower the larger double Bass.

These instruments pass out of the ordinary register of the human voice. The preliminary burr of the labial bee suggests a note on the bass fiddle but this imitation is limited and any ambition you may have to reproduce a Botte-sini solo by vocal instrumentation will never be gratified.

The sound of a double Bass can be made

by rubbing the thumb or the panel of a door,
it seems an extraordinary method to adopt and
one that has no right to be introduced here under
vocalistic effects but still you may as well
know of it.

Clench the hand so as to offer a firm support
to the thumb which, after damping slightly you
rub on panel of door following the direction in
which the thumb points. The way I find easiest
is to hold the thumb downward, and rub it downward, the dampness has the effect of rosin, and
your thumb does not glide, but makes a series
of little jerks resulting in the imitation desired.

Bassoon.

IF you make the 'cello sound and form your
lips into an O you get an imitation of this instrument. In the 'cello neither the lips nor teeth
need be closed and they are only done so for
appearance sake. In the Bassoon the lips must
form a circle, or the character is not changed
from that of the 'cello.

Cymbals.

THE imitation of the clash and clang of these
brass discs is made by a sneeze not the "ah

ah-tish-shoo" of the charwoman, but a short
sharp sneeze sent up through the nose at the
back of mouth. This imitation is very good
though it would appear to be impossible.

Drums.

THE side drum is suggested by a sharp roll of
the tongue "perr rup" "perr-rrup" "tut tut" or
"tat tat" and comes in well in imitation of Band
mixed up with other instruments. "Boom," "Perr
rrup" gives the Big Drum followed by side
Drum.

AUTOMATA.

Ventriloquial Figures, etc.

UNDER the belief that a description of the
various Talking Figures, and other automata
used in Ventriloquism would be of interest, I
submit it, as those students who think of having
a family—a Ventriloquial family—will find it a
great advantage to have particulars given them
of the various kinds that are in the market, and
their probable cost.

There may be other Figures, etc., than those
I have described, but they only differ slightly.
If the reader desires to Ventriloquize with a
Figure, and does not want to carry one about,

there are Heads, but as I have said before it is no use my advising him strongly what to do either in Ventriloquism, or choice of Automata, for he must select for himself and to do this I endeavour to assist him.

Automata.

THE man who first conceived the idea of combining Ventriloquial speech with a mouth-moving face is not even known by name, or I should have had great pleasure in mentioning it here, and complimenting him on the success of his originality, which has given employment to numerous Figure makers and to hundreds of Entertainers who would never otherwise have been able to style themselves Ventriloquists.

I saw a primitive head something like Fig. 9 which was fitted on to an upright pole, the base of which was fixed to a flange that was screwed into the stage or a stand sufficiently weighty to permit of screwing being dispensed with. This head I was told, was about the oldest in existence, and that some years ago it had taken its owner

Fig. 9.

round the world, and landed him again in England with a good sum to his credit.

That this head should lie neglected among the rubbish of a work shop, was but a confirmation of the inconstancy that is supposed to characterize the profession.

The simple man's head soon suggested a second, and the "old lady," as she is usually termed was created. They were married, and lived unhappily ever afterwards. This supposititious union, not only made the "single" man's head a "married" man's head, but permitted that wrangling over domestic matters that is supposed to constitute the principal characteristic of what is termed connubial bliss. This style of dialogue appealed to everyone, went home to them I might say, and the more the old man insulted the old lady, and the more heartily she retaliated the more did the audience enjoy the distressing incompatibility of disposition.

Flat Heads.

PROBABLY because the stands were found to be cumbersome, the Flat Heads were invented. They hung under the coat by a strap that went round the neck. When the Vent: wished to

Fig. 10.

disclose them he threw back his coat, and holding his arms akimbo rested the back of the hands on his hips and worked the mouths with his thumbs by means of a string. The surprise created by throwing back the coat, the portability, the concealment of the thumbs in working were all advantages, but the illusion that they were real was spoilt by their presentment and so they went out of favour.

Talking Hand.

THIS clever illusion is probably older than Ventriloquial Figures. If you put on a white cotton glove, and holding your hand as indicated in sketch. paint red lips on the top of thumb and lower part

Fig. 11.

of first finger; and make a nose of the first finger knuckle, and then add hair, a wig if you like, and eyes, your thumb represents the lower jaw of the Vent: Figure, and you move it accordingly

I remember seeing Mr. Verne, a capital Ventriloquist, give an excellent Interlude with a Talking Hand at the Egyptian Hall which seemed to me quite to brighten an otherwise somewhat cheerless Entertainment.

Hand Heads

ARE small heads that are held in the hand which is covered by a frill.

Fig. 12.

Knee Dolls.

THESE puppets have much to recommend them, especially for private work. The cumbersome stands, the obvious string pulling and unnatural associations are dispensed with. The Dolls can be carried in a portmanteau, and the Ventriloquist, when requested to entertain, can bring them into the room, seat himself, and have the Figures chattering on his knees before his entrance is noticed.

The position is a natural one, and the hands grasping each Figure by the neck, work the mouths with the first fingers unnoticed. When the enter-

Fig. 13.

tainment is over they are removed without trouble or loss of time, and without upsetting the room.

For Music Halls or public performances the Knee Doll is out of date, larger Figures being required by managers; though I remember some years ago a man with two Knee Dolls made a sensation in a New York Music Hall.

They are not expensive, as will be seen by the price list, and, as far as small entertainment is concerned, are most satisfactory. They are useful to begin with for practice to be exchanged afterwards for a more elaborate fit up.

Little Girl.

As a single figure this is very effective, I had one that I worked with my foot, while it stood at the piano, and sung to my accompaniment and afterwards played a violin, the sound of course being a vocal imitation, the bow arm being worked by a second pedal. Whether the girl stands, sits on the knee, or on a stool, sings, plays, recites, depends upon the special talent and business of the Ventriloquist.

Unruly Boy.

It may suit the Vent:'s humour or voice best to imitate a boy, I have seen this young gentleman

made very amusing on th
any amount of cuffing,
impertinence..

Stationary Figures: Half Size.

THESE figures are much larger than Knee Dolls
and being fixed to their seats if sitting, or to
stands if standing are capable of more extended
movement of head and neck than is possible with
Knee Dolls, where the 'Vent :'s hands are partly
employed in supporting them as well as in manipulating their mouths.

With fixed Figures
the Ventriloquist is free
to move about.

The mouth is worked
through a movable
neck from inside the
body, which allows the
head to peer about,
the neck stretched a
foot or so in any direc-
tion, or disappear as
the head is allowed

Fig. 21.

to rest close on the shoulders. The heads of the
" O.L." and " O.M." can be turned instantly towards
any sound that occurs, or in their domestic
differences their faces can be made to meet.

A back view of this style of Figure will show how easily an endless variety of movements are obtained, as it will be perceived that such movements are not limited by the extent of arranged mechanism that gives only certain effects.

The hollow body B permits the hand, working the mouth moving neck and head inside, so much freedom of action that it not only enables it to imitate every movement of the human head and neck, but supplement them by others of a grotesque character no human head and neck could ever achieve.

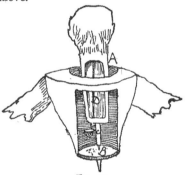

Fig. 22.

The above sketch shows the back view of a body without drapery, which of course overlaps and conceals the opening A and B without preventing the insertion of neck and head in A or performers hand in B.

The spike C is fixed on the bottom of the figure and is hidden by the dress. This spike fits loosely in the hole made in the seat upon which the Figure sits, and, being loose, the body can be made to sway about by a push with the wrist when the hand is manipulating the mouth-moving neck.

This neck is dropped into the body through the opening A in the following diagram: when the small spike B touches bottom the head is in position and will remain so.

The right hand of the performer in this Figure (which would be on his right) clutches the "clutch" C at the same time, the thumb is inserted

Fig. 23.

in the ring to the left of C, which, by a downward movement of the thumb communicates with the mouth by means of a gut string D and opens it by moving the lower jaw down, which, as soon as it is released, returns to its place by means of a spring and the mouth is closed.

It will be understood without further illustration

Q

that if C be held in the hand, any upward movement raises the head, a movement to the left causes the head to go to the right and vice versa, a turn of the wrist will turn the head round to

Fig. 24

right or left, by drawing the clutch out of body the head looks down and by pushing it into body the head looks up. Half an hour's practice with a doll of this description will give you further assurance of its powers and quite confirm anything that I have said in its favour.

The mouth-moving head and neck is detachable. and when packed fits *inside* body and wrapped in cover travels without fear of injury.

For purposes of compactness in packing the backs of bodies, heads, etc., are made *flat.* The buttons on coat are flat as otherwise in travelling they would soon wear the clothes, and besides this would not pack so well.

The arms are made to look muscular by means of rings sewn inside the sleeves, as is done with Marionette Figures. When the Figures sit, the Box they travel in is often used in various ways for the purpose, when covered with a bright cover.

The disadvantage of the majority of sitting Figures that utilize their own boxes, is that this arrangement covers up the performer, a matter I have preached against before when referring to stage dressing,* and compels him to give his Entertainment as a shop man sells neckties—from behind a counter.

To these two figures you rely for the back bone of your Entertainment, and additions must be made with care, or you will soon have a lot of puppets not worth the trouble of carrying about.

PART V.

CONCLUSION.

HAVING accompanied me so far the reader will understand, especially if he have ever before tried to study Ventriloquism from books, the reason of my seeming punctiliousness in regard to classification. It was, the only way I could say clearly what this art of imitating near or distant sounds was. The reader now has no more confusion on the subject than I have, and can arrange an Entertainment to suit his fancy and know exactly of what materials he is building it.

It appears a very easy matter to lay down a few simple rules, and reduce all relevant matter to comprehensibility but it is not so in an art in which its study and its apprehension is in a chaotic state, its nomenclature false and its true character perverted by careless or intentionally misleading statements from the stage and published anecdotes that further the general misunderstanding about it.

In teaching I have always endeavoured to lay a foundation, to create a correct taste, and serve my pupils with a reasonable method of study, not merely say by doing this you imitate so and so, but by acquiring this you can employ it for all sounds of a certain class, thus certain rules become known and the varieties of sounds distant, near, reedy, vibratory, etc., are easily conquered because the method is understood and immediately employed to realize the required effect.

I became fascinated with Ventriloquism and it was the recollection of the difficulty of obtaining instruction, and its rudimentary character when obtained, that made me determined to formulate some reliable method, to which end I have given years of study to produce an exhaustive and practical treatise on this art.

For my part I am convinced that the more known of the marvellous power of the human voice the more will it be admired, not for what it cannot do, but for what it can do, if properly trained.

Ingram Content Group UK Ltd.
Milton Keynes UK
UKHW041835180523
421997UK00002B/7